INSIGHT POCKET GUIDE

CaIRnS &
The GReaT
BaRRIeR ReeF

Discovery
CHANNEL

APA PUBLICATIONS
Part of the Langenscheidt Publishing Group

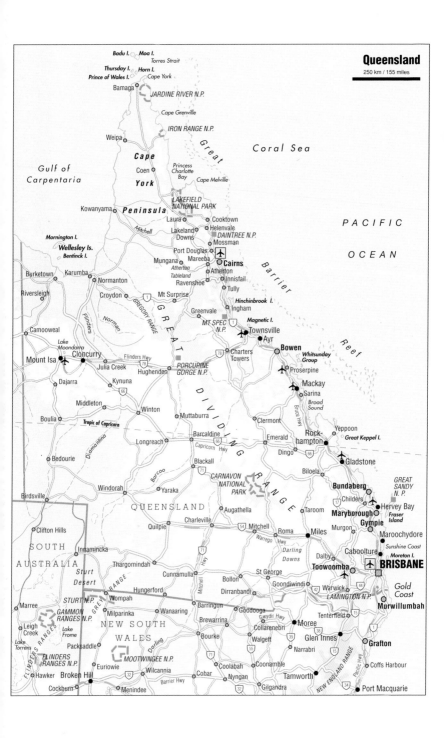

Queensland

250 km / 155 miles

Welcome

T his guidebook combines the interests and enthusiasms of two of the world's best-known information providers: Insight Guides, who have set the standard for visual travel guides since 1970, and Discovery Channel, the world's premier source of non-fiction television programming. Its aim is to bring you the best of Cairns and the Great Barrier Reef in a series of itineraries devised by Insight's Australia correspondent, Paul Phelan.

Queensland, the sunshine state, is the most visited place in Australia after Sydney. And it is to Cairns, gateway to the Great Barrier Reef, that many visitors are drawn. The city – capital of Tropical North Queensland – has its share of attractions, but its real jewels are found inland and in the cobalt seas bordering it. The first eight itineraries in this guide use Cairns (and nearby beaches like Palm Cove or Port Douglas) as a base to venture into millennia-old rainforests and dramatic plateaus carved by volcanic activity, as well as explore sandy beaches and snorkel on the incredible Great Barrier Reef. This is followed by five excursions to Cape York Peninsula and farther flung beaches and islands: Mission and Airlie beaches, and Dunk, Whitsunday and Heron islands, plus a cruise along the Coral Coast.

Complementing the itineraries in this guide are chapters on outdoor activities, shopping, eating out and nightlife, and a fact-packed practical information section covering all the travel essentials you need to know.

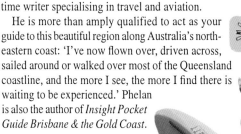

Paul Phelan moved to Queensland over 30 years ago when he worked as an airline pilot. He moved to Cairns 10 years later, and attracted by Tropical North Queensland's great diversity and natural beauty, and by the earthy good humour and natural friendliness of its people, Phelan soon found himself developing and managing a new holiday resort at the tip of remote Cape York. He is now a full-time writer specialising in travel and aviation.

He is more than amply qualified to act as your guide to this beautiful region along Australia's north-eastern coast: 'I've now flown over, driven across, sailed around or walked over most of the Queensland coastline, and the more I see, the more I find there is waiting to be experienced.' Phelan is also the author of *Insight Pocket Guide Brisbane & the Gold Coast*.

6   **contents**

forest World Heritage Site, lush Mena Creek Falls and Mission Beach, jump-off point for Dunk, a tropical island with bush walking, swimming and snorkelling **51**

2   Cruising the Coral Coast is a four-night cruise that follows the course of Captain Cook's voyage, calling at Fitzroy Island and Cooktown, before heading out to the coral cays and islands of the Great Barrier Reef **55**

3   Cape York Peninsula involves a four-wheel-drive exploration of the Outback in the remote north, past Lakeland Downs and Black Mountain to historic Cooktown and back down the coastal road **59**

4   The Whitsunday Islands is further down the Queensland coast. Using Airlie Beach on mainland as a base, explore the crystal-clear waters, white sand beaches and the coral reefs of nearby islands, including Hamilton **64**

5   Heron Island is a true coral island on the Tropic of Capricorn. Learn about the ecosystems of the Great Barrier Reef, and experience some of the best diving in the world, plus lots of land-based attractions **69**

LEISURE ACTIVITIES

A list of exciting outdoor activities, and tips on what to buy, where to eat, and where to stay up late **73–85**

CALENDAR OF EVENTS

A guide to festivals and events in the Cairns area **86**

PRACTICAL INFORMATION

All the background information you are likely to need for your stay, from taxis to tipping and customs to currency, including a list of recommended hotels **89–99**

MAPS

CREDITS AND INDEX

Pages 2/3: snorkellers, with MV *Reef Endeavour* in the distance
Pages 8/9: picturesque Centenary Lakes in Cairns

History & *Culture*

rusty, conservative and controversial former Queensland Premier, Sir Johannes Bjelke-Petersen, once announced with pride that some 60,000 people were immigrating to Queensland annually from the southern states in search of a better future. His critics in Melbourne and Sydney promptly declared that this was a great benefit to the nation as it increased the average IQ levels in all three states. *Touché.*

Northern Queensland was a late starter in the race to bring European civilisation, culture and economics into Australia. In fact, the process only began about 100 years after the first Europeans settled in the southeast – but Queenslanders say they have achieved the same progress in half the time. The rapidity of the state's development has shaped its society and its attitudes.

Captain Cook's Landing

The voyage of 18th-century maritime explorer Captain James Cook, who sailed up the length of Australia's east coast, was European civilisation's first recorded hint of a vast territory filled with opportunity and promise. Over the previous two centuries, French, Dutch, Portuguese and Spanish navigators landed on the island continent, but they had all approached from the west, encountered arid and inhospitable tracts of coastline, and returned with unflattering assessments of the land and its native inhabitants.

Returning in 1770 from an expedition to Tahiti, Cook could hardly have chosen a more promising point of first contact on the mainland – on what is now New South Wales' south coast – to begin his northward voyage of exploration. He found a temperate climate, fertile soil, ample water, promising harbours and a primitive population of hunter-gatherers who had never farmed the land and consequently had not been able to exploit its potential.

To Cook, the maze of coral shoals now known as the Great Barrier Reef were no more than a detested obstacle, which almost robbed him of his ship, his crew and his life. Nor was he greeted by inhabitants eager for trade and cultural exchange. Although there is scattered but convincing evidence that earlier civilisations had gained fleeting footholds on the island continent, the only surviving culture when Cook arrived was that of the Aboriginal tribes.

In the arid interior, the Aborigines were nomadic because food and water were scarce, and its search unrelenting. Along the coast and adjacent ranges, however, the native population was less transient because food and water were more plentiful. The boundaries of these tribal groups were therefore more defined.

CAPTAIN JAMES COOK
1728 ~ 1779
COMMANDER. H.M.B. "ENDEAVOUR"
WHICH WAS BEACHED AND REPAIRED
NEAR THIS SITE 17 JUNE - 4 AUGUST, 1770.
"HE LEFT NOTHING UNATTEMPTED."
THIS STATUE WAS COMMISSIONED BY
BP AUSTRALIA AS A BICENTENNIAL GIFT
TO THE PEOPLE OF COOKTOWN
AND UNVEILED BY MR. A.W. GORRIE
CHAIRMAN OF THE BOARD.
SATURDAY, 25 JUNE 1988.
SCULPTOR: STANLEY HAMMOND M.B.E.

Left: early European impression of an Aboriginal camp
Right: Captain Cook made his first landing in 1770

Colonisation

Cook claimed the continent in the name of the British Crown, but little was done to develop the land until the War of Independence forced Britain to stop shipping convicts to America. As a result, the first fleet that sailed into Sydney Cove on 13 May 1787 carried convicts and scarlet-jacketed soldiers rather than settlers, builders or miners.

Its harbour and hinterland made Sydney the obvious choice for a first settlement. The newcomers then worked their way northward, and Brisbane, about midway up the east coast, was the last major colonial port to be established – again as a penal colony. Almost the entire Queensland coast thus remained open for exploration, which began to progress in earnest only after the settlement in the southeast corner was properly established.

The Displaced Aborigines

Queensland's first European settlements were established wherever suitable harbours were found on the coast, to support the agricultural, mining and logging industries of the interior as well as for coastal trading. There is no question that the settlers, miners and explorers showed poor regard for Aboriginal feelings or territories.

Conflicts sprang up endlessly over what the settlers considered to be the theft of their animals and stores by Aborigines, which the natives simply regarded as hunting and gathering. As the European population increased, many Aborigines were marginalised to become fringe dwellers around the settlements, although many proved to be excellent horsemen and livestock handlers.

In 1848, explorer Edmond Kennedy and a party of 12 men landed at Tam O'Shanter Point, near Dunk Island, in search of a way through the ranges behind the coast, intending to travel to the tip of Cape York. His progress was impeded first by swamps and disease, and later by disagreements with Aborigines. Although Kennedy found the inland route less inhospitable than along the densely-vegetated and more mountainous east coast, everyone in his party died along the way except one Aboriginal companion. Kennedy himself was fatally speared only miles away from his goal.

On 6 June 1859, Queen Victoria signed the Letters Patent allowing Queensland to separate from the New South Wales colony, an event now celebrated each year as Queensland Day, which focuses on the state's history and development, as well as the achievements of Queenslanders. Sir George Ferguson Bowen was appointed Queensland's first Governor.

Above: Aborigines performing the traditional *corroboree* dance

Goldfields and New Seaports

Almost 100 years after Cook's voyage, prospector James Mulligan found gold on the Palmer River, and Cooktown came into being as a seaport and supply link for the new goldfields. In March 1876, gold was also found to the south of the Palmer on the Hodgkinson River, 100km (62 miles) inland, and the need for another port became apparent. In July, magistrate Brinsley Guise Sheridan was sent to report on the suitability of Trinity Inlet, and Cooktown storekeepers began preparing goods for shipment as soon as the new port was opened.

In August 1876, some Townsville businessmen chartered the steamer *Porpoise* and arrived in Trinity Bay to find a small fleet already in possession. Among them was the stern paddle steamer *Louisa*, belonging to a Herbert River sugar plantation owner and the *Fairy*, with men from Cooktown and *bêche-de-mer* (sea cucumber) fisherman. The *Porpoise* sailed 20km (12½ miles) up Smiths Creek at the head of Trinity Inlet and attempts were made to explore the country, but swamps, tangled mangroves and an Aboriginal war party forced them to give up the expedition.

In spite of these tribulations, the new town of Cairns – named after the then Governor of Queensland, Sir William Wellington Cairns – was established as a port of entry on 1 November 1876. Once again gold had in a few months brought about developments which would otherwise have taken years. Gold diggers and packers using the Hodgkinson River soon realised they could save 30km (18½ miles) of boggy travel and find good grass for their horses by sailing up the Barron River – until they were stopped by fierce rapids.

A camp was established there; pub and shanty keepers moved in, and soon Smithfield, named after explorer Bill Smith, had a larger population than Cairns. Unfortunately, every time the Barron River flooded, Smithfield became inundated with water. Another reason for its decline was that yet another new port had been established further up the coast, when adventurer and explorer Christie Palmerston discovered an easier route from the coast to the goldfields. The new Port Douglas was declared a port of entry in 1877.

Agriculture and Industry

Sugar cane, rice, timber and cattle were among the first industries to take hold in the region, but as settlements sprang up, prospectors used them as bases from which they found gold and later tin, bauxite, wolfram, copper and other minerals. And in the Torres Strait, pearl shell and *bêche-de-mer*, the sea cucumber prized by the Chinese as a delicacy, were also discovered and exploited.

At first Governor Cairns paid little attention to the tent city carrying his name, but in 1879, after his departure, the first local authority was established in the area, and in 1884 Cairns was declared a municipal borough. A significant event in the town's history was the government's decision to build a much-needed railway from the coast to the Atherton Tablelands.

Right: *The Prospector*, an 1889 painting by Julian Ashton captures the aspirations of the early settlers

Cairns, Gordonvale, Innisfail and Port Douglas all competed for the privilege of having the coastal terminus of the line, but, despite the daunting terrain that would have to be tackled, Cairns won the day. The construction began in 1886, using mainly Italian and Irish workers. Many of them died of disease and injury, but many more survived and went on to become farmers and businessmen. Notably, many generations of people of Italian descent have dominated the sugar cane industry.

Sugar cane made its first appearance at Cairns in 1881, and a year later, tea and coffee were first planted at Bingil Bay, near Mission Beach. In those early days, the development of such primary industries brought huge demands for labour in the sugar cane fields, as well as to harvest *bêche-de-mer* from the sea, to dive for pearls and to work in the mines.

In times when the law of the jungle prevailed, it was all too easy for some brigand to sail a schooner into the Pacific and force an island chieftain to accept a gallon of rum for his aid in recruiting 'indentured' labour for the cane fields. To be fair, these shady deals included a modest remuneration and food and lodgings for the worker, and repatriation at the end of the contract. Large numbers of 'recruited' South Sea Islanders decided to stay on, and many more returned to work by choice. Likewise, the pearlers and bêche-de-mer traders also showed little conscience in their recruitment practices in the Torres Strait and Cape York Peninsula's east coast.

Federation and Conflict

Until Federation in 1901, when Queensland's population was around 502,000, New South Wales, Victoria, Western Australia, South Australia and Tasmania were independent colonies, operating by their own rules. Disputes were common among them on defence, immigration, communications, trade and tariffs – even railway gauges. It became increasingly clear that a better way forward for the continent had to be found, and Federation brought the colonies together to form a united Australia. Australians take such a keen interest in the shaping of their destiny that, since the Constitution was framed in 1901, 44 proposals to change it have been put to the population in referenda – and only eight have received the necessary mandate.

For many Australians, the advent of World War II was the first time Far North Queensland ever came to their notice. The battle of the Coral Sea – the first major carrier-to-carrier naval battle of World War II – which took place from 4–8 May 1942, was fought between a combined Australian-American force and the Japanese naval and air forces just off the North Queensland coast. Then, in late July 1942, Japanese long-range flying boats raided North Queensland, dropping bombs in the Mossman area, and an invasion seemed to be on the cards. Royal Australian Air Force radar stations were set up,

Above: Pacific islanders labouring in the cane fields of the Queensland coast, circa 1900
Right: the Great Barrier Reef, accursed by sailors in Cook's day, is a treasured asset today

and concealed 'coastwatchers' were positioned along the coast to Cape York. Atherton's Barron Valley Hotel was used as headquarters for part of the war and thousands of troops were camped in the area for jungle warfare training. The Japanese invasion never materialised.

Post-War Development

Two world wars and over 130 years of high-volume settlement by diverse migrants from Europe and Asia have helped develop Cairns into a thriving tropical city, with an economy initially based on the sugar, mining and dairy industries. In the first half of the 20th century, because Australia had been busy developing the economy of the new Federated territory, there was little recognition of the potential offered by the Great Barrier Reef, which stretches some 2,300km (1,430 miles) along the Queensland coast. Prior to 1900, over 600 shipwrecks had been recorded on the reef. These included the *Pandora*, which, returning to England from Tahiti with 14 captured mutineers from the HMS *Bounty*, struck coral while attempting to pass through the outer reef.

In the intervening years, safe routes and a shipping pilot service have been established to provide safe passage for the transit of merchant ships and countless fishing and pleasure vessels every year. And in the post-war years, with more leisure time on their hands, Australians began to take notice of the reef and the region's tropical coastline and hinterland. No longer were rainforests something to be torn down for timber and the land exploited for agriculture; and no longer was the Great Barrier Reef nothing but a nuisance to shipping and an unlimited source of delicious seafood.

Growth of Tourism

The advent of jet aircraft, which transformed Cairns from its early 'colonial outpost' status to that of a premier port of entry, was boosted further in March 1984 when its airport was given international status. As the centre of tourist activity in the area, Cairns has largely been taken over by high-rise hotels and shopping malls, but you can find fine examples of traditional buildings made from the wood of cedar and silky oak trees. The advent of electric fans and air conditioning, and the increasing price and

scarcity of timber, have since transformed construction, but some of the trademarks, such as timber lattice, have survived in modern buildings, imparting a distinctive Queensland architectural style.

But there have been ecological disasters too. In 1935, cane toads were introduced into the Gordonvale area south of Cairns from Hawaii in order to combat the sugar cane beetle which was destroying precious cane crops. The beetle, however, inhabited the flowers and seeds 1.8m (6ft) above the ground and beyond the reach of the terrestrial cane toad, which has now hopped all over Queensland and become a pest in about half of Australia. The hated creature does, however, provide sport for Cairns motorists on wet, humid nights.

Melting Pot

The region's lawless past is behind it, and its natural beauty and economic strength have assured its future. Queensland's population is now 3.6 million, with over 20 percent of Cairns' 130,000 population born overseas. Indigenous languages are almost as culturally diverse as the population. Many Aborigines and Torres Straits Islanders use a form of pidgin when speaking among themselves, while the Italian- and Greek-speaking communities make up two of the largest and oldest population groups in the region. Polish, Spanish, Croatian, Dutch, German, Russian, Swiss and South Americans are fewer in number but significantly represented. Most speak English fluently.

Cairns also has a growing refugee community from the former Yugoslavia, Sudan, West Papua and Iraq. South Pacific Islander groups from Papua New Guinea, East Timor, Fiji, the Cook Islands, Samoa, Tonga and Maori New Zealanders are among the fastest growing language groups, while there is also significant immigration from Japan, Malaysia, India and Indonesia.

The intermingling of cultures has enriched every aspect of the region's culture – which is nowhere more evident than in the markets that flourish at all major (and many minor) centres, and in the variety of its places of religious worship. And undeterred by comments about their IQ, the internal migrants from the south, as well as from other countries, continue to arrive.

Above: Pacific Islander immigrants weaving a mat at Fogarty Park, Cairns

HISTORY HIGHLIGHTS

1770 Captain James Cook explores Australia's east coast.

1787 The first fleet sails into Sydney Cove on 13 May, loaded with convicts and marines.

1802 Explorer Matthew Flinders in HMS *Investigator* sails through the Whitsunday Passage and charts the inner edge of the Great Barrier Reef.

1825 A convict settlement is established on the site of Brisbane, now the state capital.

1848 Edmund Kennedy sets out from Tam O'Shanter Point to chart a land route up the Cape York Peninsula.

1864 The Jardine brothers set out from the Burnett region to drive a herd of cattle and horses to the tip of remote Cape York.

1868 Queensland's pearling industry is established in the Torres Straits.

1873 James Mulligan discovers payable gold on the Palmer River and receives an award of £1,000 from the government.

1876 Gold is found on the Hodgkinson River. A party reaches Trinity Bay and the new town of Cairns is proclaimed a port of entry to serve the mining industry from Trinity Inlet.

1877 Adventurer Christie Palmerston discovers an easier route from the goldfields to the coast, and Port Douglas is declared a port of entry.

1880 Tin is discovered in Herberton.

1882 Tea and coffee are first planted at Bingil Bay, and sugar cane at Gordonvale.

1884 Cairns is declared a municipal borough.

1885 Legislation is passed to discontinue the 'recruiting' of Pacific islanders for Queensland's tropical agriculture, to be implemented over the next five years.

1891 The Cairns to Kuranda railway line is completed.

1896 The first sugar cane is crushed at the Mulgrave Central Mill at Gordonvale, south of Cairns.

1901 Australia's six independent colonies are federated into the Commonwealth of Australia under a common constitution.

1920 Passenger ships offer one-day stopovers on a Whitsunday 'tropical island', heralding the area's success as a tourism destination.

1926 The Cairns to Yungaburra range road (now Gillies Highway) is opened.

1929 The first Whitsunday resort is established on Lindeman Island.

1942 Japanese planes attack Pearl Harbor in the USA and later Darwin. Australian naval bases are established at Cairns and Thursday Island. The Battle of the Coral Sea is fought from 4–8 May. Catalina flying boats operating from Cairns attack Japanese positions in the Pacific islands.

1947 Airline owner Reg Ansett introduces big business into the Whitsundays with acquisition of Hayman Island.

1951 Bush Pilots Airways, established to open up communications and transport on Cape York, makes its first scheduled flight.

1976 The Great Barrier Reef Marine Park Authority is established, with responsibility for protecting the extensive coral reefs.

1984 Cairns International Airport is opened. A track, negotiable only by off-road vehicles, is opened up between Cape Tribulation and Bloomfield River amid considerable protest.

1988 World Heritage status is accorded to 900,000ha (2¼ million acres) of North Queensland's tropical rainforests.

1992 The Australian High Court rejects the *Terra Nullus* (empty land) concept which had existed since the time of European discovery, and instead rules that the native title has survived the annexation of the country.

2001 Centenary of the Australian Federation.

2003 Development of Cairns foreshore as a centre of visitor leisure activity is completed.

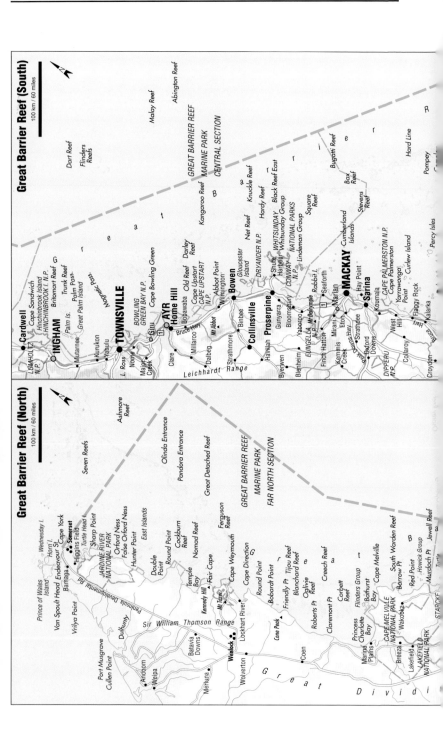

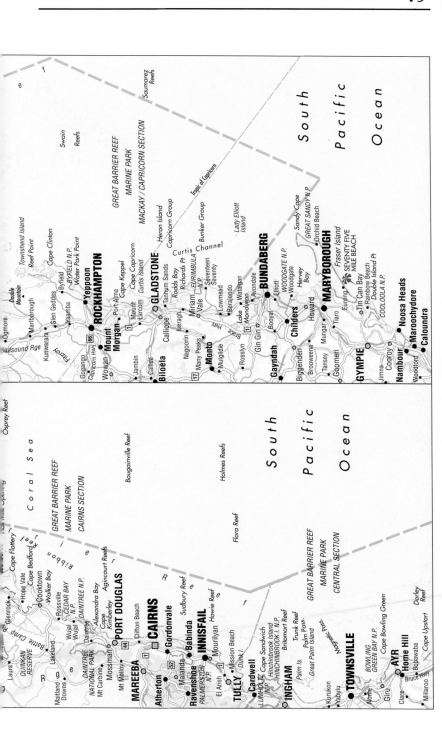

Orientation

Tropical North Queensland occupies the far northeast corner of Australia, and its greatest treasures are the Great Barrier Reef and the Wet Tropics rainforest – both designated as World Heritage Sites. The Great Barrier Reef – which includes some 2,900 individual reefs, 300 coral cays and more than 1,000 islands – spans over 350,000sq km (135,000sq miles) in area. It stretches for 2,300km (1,430 miles) off the east coast of Queensland in the aptly named Coral Sea, and up here in the Tropical North is where it is closest to the shore. Some 80km (50 miles) wide in places, the reef and its coral islands form a wonderland of marine life. And along the mainland shore is a succession of white-sand beaches backed by lush rainforest.

Stretching back from the coast, and extending to over 9,000sq km (3,500sq miles), the Wet Tropics rainforest is the oldest of its kind in the world, and with the greatest diversity of endemic species. Further south, rolling inland towards the Great Dividing Range, are the Atherton Tablelands, with fertile pastures and cattle stations, country towns, and scenic lakes and waterfalls. And beyond this lies the Outback and the old mining settlements.

Cairns, on Trinity Bay, is perfectly placed for exploring everything the Tropical North has to offer, both on and offshore. Backed by forested hills, it's a compact town right on the main coastal highway, with most of the action found around the Esplanade area. One thing to remember if you're coming from the northern hemisphere is that the seasons are in reverse here – Christmas is in mid-summer – and the orientation is opposite, with the water spiralling down the plug-hole the opposite way.

Cairns, Palm Cove or Port Douglas?

This book contains eight itineraries that each occupy a whole day, followed by five excursions for longer trips, (including a cruise), which incorporate overnight stops along the way. Cairns is the most obvious choice as a base for a North Queensland holiday because it has the main transport links, including an international airport, railway and long-distance bus connections, along with a plethora of holiday accommodation, nightlife, restaurants and shopping outlets.

Because of this, however, Cairns has become rather built-up and can be too boisterous for some – and it doesn't have a beach – so you may prefer to base yourself at Palm Cove, Port Douglas, Mission Beach or other smaller beachside resorts along the Tropical North Queensland coast. Wherever you stay, you will need to hire a car (possibly a four-wheel-drive) for most of the trips in this guide, except for Excursions 4 and 5, to which you will be flying to.

Left: Kuranda Scenic Railway on Stony Creek bridge
Right: the always adorable koala

1. EXPLORING CAIRNS *(see map below)*

A coastal and rainforest walk with tropical scenery and elevated views across the city, taking in the Esplanade, Botanical Gardens, Tanks Art Centre and Royal Flying Doctor Service Visitor Centre.

Start at the pathway opposite the Sofitel Reef Casino on the seafront side of the Hilton Hotel. You could get around this itinerary in a half-day, but it can more comfortably fill a whole day, so set out right after breakfast and take your time. If it's too hot or wet, or if your time is limited, you could spend a rewarding half-day on horticulturalist Andrew Doyle's Cairns Discovery Tour (City Sights Plus; tel: 07 4053 5259; www.cairnsdiscoveries.com.au).

From the boardwalk along the sea wall you'll see dozens of yachts and powered craft moored in the enclosed marina and along the opposite shore, many occupied by people who have sailed into Cairns en route to somewhere else, become addicted to the city's relaxed lifestyle, and decided to stay on.

The Esplanade Area

Keep to the shoreline path to the right of the hotel and **Pier Marketplace** shopping complex, overlooking the marina. Around the corner is a huge, usually crowded, landscaped swimming lagoon, with a walkway along the

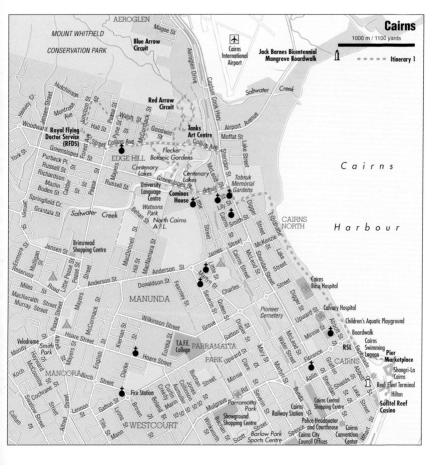

sea wall. This area, and the rest of the **Esplanade**, including an aquatic children's playground, is the hub of Cairns activity and a window on its relaxed lifestyle.

Much of the coastal parkland is on reclaimed ground. At high tide, the water laps the narrow beach all the way along the shoreline, and that's when the brochure photographs are taken. When it recedes, Cairns' famous and not unattractive mud flats are exposed. The mud, dumped during World War II when the shipping channel was dredged, has spread across the bay's shallows and is rich in marine life. This has created a new home for hundreds of water birds, some of which migrate from as far away as Siberia.

Two ancient artillery pieces are mounted in front of the **Returned Servicemen's League** (RSL) building, commemorating Cairns' key role in the Battle of the Coral Sea in 1942. A little further along, near the tennis courts and atop a tall plinth, you'll see a commemorative model of the famous Catalina flying boat, a frequent visitor to Trinity Inlet during the conflict. From their base at Cairns, these remarkable aircraft flew patrols of up to 24 hours, locating and attacking ships of the Japanese fleet.

Indigenous Vegetation

At the northern end of the pathway you'll have walked about 2.5km (1½ miles). Pass behind the childrens' playground ship and continue along the parallel Esplanade for another block, turn left, and when you reach the sports ground a block further on, walk diagonally across it (unless the hockey sticks are flying) to pass the Tobruk Pool on your right. At the lights, cross Sheridan Street into Arthur Street, which becomes Greenslopes Street after a couple of blocks, then go over the railway crossing and Lily Creek bridge. On the next corner is **Cominos House**, a typical colonial-style home on stilts that was the residence of one of Cairns' earliest settler families until1988. Relocated from its original Abbot Street site, it has been adapted into an environmental and arts centre.

Opposite the house and on your right is a path into the **Flecker Botanic Gardens**, which consist of three main areas: the **Centenary Lakes** where you are now, the main botanic gardens (Mon–Fri 7.30am–5.30pm, weekends and public holidays 8.30am–5.30pm; tel: 07 4044 3398), and the **Mount Whitfield Conservation Park**.

You're first treated to a shady park with a small salt-water lake to your left, a waterfowl habitat that is worth a pause. This area is a tidied-up version of the original countryside, with predominantly native trees typical of the vegetation of low-lying

Above: the Esplanade's sprawling swimming lagoon
Right: tranquil Centenary Lakes

coastal land in the region. From a footbridge across the mangrove-lined **Salt-water Creek**, imagine the daunting environment that first challenged early explorers who ventured up the crocodile infested waterway by boat.

Just after the bridge, take the right fork on the concrete path and then the left fork a little further on. Don't be distracted by a sign to the Rainforest Boardwalk, which we're saving for later. The bush on your left now more closely represents the undisturbed original, with huge swamp paper-barks and other native species (many of them labelled) which attracted the early loggers.

The Red Arrow Walk

You'll soon emerge onto Collins Avenue opposite the **Tanks Art Centre**, converted wartime fuel tanks that are now used as premises for temporary art exhibitions, usually with local themes. Hours vary, so call 07 4032 2349 for information.

Walk along Collins Avenue to a small off-street parking bay on the right, which is the beginning of the **Red Arrow Walk**. A well-made but steep walking track leads you to tranquil gullies, through virgin rainforest, and to sweeping viewpoints that look out over the town centre, Trinity Bay, the airport, and the mangrove creeks and swamps along the coastline. When you come to a fork in the track, take the left path – the walk goes around a loop from this point, returning down the other path. At the top of the ridge, take the right fork (the left one is the more strenuous Blue Arrow circuit) and along the spur you'll find a covered shelter overlooking the airport – a great place to rest awhile and enjoy the scenery. On the return path there are fine views of the city.

Back at the car park, turn right up Collins Avenue and in a few hundred metres you'll reach the **Botanic Gardens** proper. It will probably be lunchtime by now, and the **Botanic Gardens Restaurant** (daily 8.30am–4.30pm; tel: 07 4053 7087) in the grounds is ideally placed (if you are packing this itinerary into a half-day, just have a cup of tea here and press on).

Suitably refreshed, take some time to wander through the more formal part of the gardens surrounding you, which are rich in both indigenous and exotic species. At the gardens' office, pick up a walk leaflet or an audio-tour (in several languages). The gardens contain most of the timber species that first drew the white population to Cairns, including Queensland cedar and several varieties of silky oak, which polishes to a hologram-like finish and forms the structure of many of the older homes.

Above: signage, Tanks Arts Centre
Left: palm fruit at the Botanic Gardens
Right: mural, Royal Flying Doctor Service

Flying Doctor Service

From the gardens, walk up McCormack Street, which runs off Collins Avenue to the west, and turn left into Walsh Street. Here you can catch some fascinating glimpses of what became the city's first 'upper-crust' suburb, **Edge Hill**, where much of its distinctive architectural style developed. Turn left again into Junction Street, and on your right just before the street bends to the left, you'll arrive at the **Royal Flying Doctor Service** (Mon–Sat 9am–4.30pm; tel: 07 4053 5687; www.flyingdoctorqueensland.net).

Over 80 years ago, Dr John Flynn, a missionary in the remote interior, saw a need to bring modern health and emergency medical services to what was then the far-flung Outback. Using vintage planes and primitive communications based on pedal-driven radios, the Flying Doctor Service became a vital link between the Outback and the major population centres. It brought not only emergency services but also health advice, 'telegram' communications and what is now known as distance education. The latter allowed children to communicate with their educators and fellow students from their remote homes. The sense of community that the service helped to enhance is one of the most inspiring stories of Australia's inland development. A video, 'A Day in the Life of the Flying Doctor', brings the story to life.

Back on the road, it's just a short walk around the corner and along Fleming Street, and a right turn takes you to the Edge Hill roundabout. You can stop for afternoon tea (or lunch if you are doing this itinerary in half-day) at **Mandy's Continental Deli Café** (Avenue Shopping Centre, 86 Woodward Street; tel: 07 4032 5643), which is popular with the locals.

Walk back along Collins Avenue to the Botanic Gardens and take the path opposite the main entrance, which leads to the **Rainforest Boardwalk**. This elevated walkway keeps your feet dry as you pass through otherwise untouched lowland rainforest, with its giant paperbark trees, pandanus and indigenous palm species. At the end of the boardwalk is a freshwater lake with waterlilies, bounded on two sides by the swampy rainforest that has deterred interference by man since colonisation. The best way to return to the central business district is the way you came – along the Esplanade.

2. PORT DOUGLAS AND MOSSMAN GORGE
(see map, below & p28)

Sail and swim or just take it easy on famous Four Mile Beach at the chic resort of Port Douglas, then explore scenic Mossman Gorge.

Wherever you are based, the Captain Cook Highway will bring you to the Port Douglas turn-off. From Cairns you need to go north past the Smithfield roundabout and continue for 64km (40 miles), taking a right turn onto Port Douglas Road. As the road curves left, turn right into Barrier Street for the south end of Four Mile Beach. Bring swimming gear and sun protection, and suitable clothing for afternoon tea at the Sheraton.

Not very long ago, **Port Douglas** was a sleepy seaside settlement. Today, it has been transformed into a fashionable tropical holiday resort and retirement township, with the whole spectrum of tourist accommodation and attendant diversions. Fortunately, the transition has not robbed Port Douglas of its natural charms.

The approach from the main road is an early clue to the town's evolution. It is lined by an avenue of about 450 huge African oil palms, and as many again are planted around the Sheraton Mirage Resort and the Marina Mirage – part of the extravagant vision of former multi-millionaire Christopher Skase, who went spectacularly bust in a series of Australian and international media and leisure ventures. About 1,500 palm trees were transplanted here in the

Above: Port Douglas' famous Four Mile Beach

mid 1980s at a cost of about AU\$1,500 each. Happily, Port Douglas fared better than its benefactor, and it has continued to survive and prosper.

Four Mile Beach

Four Mile Beach is the town's prime asset. Once backed by nothing but hinterland swamp, it still retains an air of spacious solitude – unless you peer through the bush and discover cabanas where crocodiles once lurked. Take the pathway near the southern end of the beach, the least crowded part, where the temptation might be to simply crash out on the sands and soak up the sun – or you could stroll the 4km (2½ miles) to the northern end (and maybe get a taxi back). Swimming is safe, but stay inside the nets in the stinger season (these nasty box jellyfish infest the waters offshore from October to May). Another possibility is to hire a catamaran, sea kayak or double surf skis (Port Douglas Water Sports; Mar–Nov daily 9am–5pm, weather permitting; tel: 0404 856 821), and test your skill at skimming the blue water.

Next, get back in the car and retrace your route to Port Douglas Road, turning right for the drive up to the 'central business district', where souvenir and beach fashion shops compete for your attention and your dollars. Browse for a while, then drive to the parkland fronting the water. Turn right up Wharf Street, a steep hill containing some of Port Douglas' most expensive residences, to reach **Lookout Point**. From here, there are sweeping views over Four Mile Beach and the coastline, extending most of the way to Cairns and the mountains beyond. You can also see Skase's centrepiece, now the **Sheraton Mirage Resort** and **Marina Mirage**, the boating-cum-shopping complex he built on reclaimed mangrove swamp.

For a delicious lunch, get an outside table at the waterside seafood restaurant, **On The Inlet** (3 Inlet Street; tel: 07 4099 5255), where most of the seafood is local – try the warm prawn cappacio.

If you need a change from seafood, drop by at **Mocca's Pies**, a local institution of considerable fame and (takeaway) talent at 9 Warner Street, 9am–3pm or until sold out.

Mossman Gorge and the Rainforest Sanctuary

Drive back down Wharf Street and take the main road south from Port Douglas to meet the Captain Cook Highway. You will pass the Rainforest Habitat Wildlife Sanctuary, but keep going – we'll be returning here later. At the main road turn right, and it's only a 21-km (13-mile) drive north to Mossman. Turn left here and follow the signs for another 5km (3 miles) to **Mossman Gorge**, passing through sugar cane fields and later rainforest to reach the **Mossman River**.

From the car park here, you can access the swimming area a little way upstream, either along a well-made path through the bush or an only slightly less easy one along the river bank beside the roaring rapids. Swimming in the cool, clear water among the rocks is safe, but excercise caution. Just a little further up

Right: Mossman River Gorge

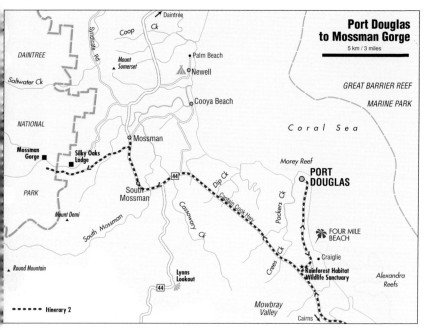

the path is a suspension bridge leading to a 2.7-km (1½-mile) walking circuit through the rainforest, with interpretive signs detailing many of the plant species growing there, and how they are used by the Aboriginal Kuku Yalanji people and various forest animals.

When you have seen enough, head back towards Port Douglas; just after turning off the Captain Cook Highway look for signs for the **Rainforest Habitat Wildlife Sanctuary** (daily 8am–5.30pm; tel: 07 4099 3235; www.rainforesthabitat.com.au) on the left. It offers a chance to observe up close over 180 species of flora and fauna in four environments: rainforest, wetlands, woodlands and grasslands.

In the rainforest you'll see native species such as Boyd's forest dragon, eclectus parrots, red-tailed black cockatoos and green tree frogs in a natural setting. A meandering walkway allows you to experience different levels of the rainforest from ground level to high in the canopy. In the wetlands, an array of wading birds can be viewed foraging for fish and crustacea in waterways that wind their way beneath boardwalks and pathways, while the grasslands entice you to interact with a range of macropods from the statuesque Eastern Grey kangaroo to the petite Parma wallaby.

The billabong is home to turtles, frogs and a range of waterfowl while also attracting a host of native birds; over 40 species using the area for breeding have been recorded. Estuarine and freshwater crocodiles lurk beneath the murky waters or bask on the sunlit banks. Last is the koala habitat, which provides visitors with an eye-level view of this unusual marsupial.

Before winding down for the day, indulge in an elegant high tea at the luxury **Sheraton Mirage Resort** (daily 3–5pm, tel: 07 4099 5888). It's wise to book in advance for this treat at the opulent Daintree Lounge.

3. KURANDA SCENIC CIRCUIT *(see map, p32)*

Travel to picturesque Kuranda on the scenic railway, buy a souvenir from a hippie turned capitalist, and return to Cairns on the 'Skyrail' cable car, skimming tropical rainforest and waterfalls along the way.

Get to Cairns Central Station in time to catch the 8.30am train (which also stops at Freshwater station at 8.45am). Book the rail and cableway package with Skyrail (tel: 07 4038 1555; www.skyrail.com.au). You'll also need to decide on a departure time from Kuranda – 2 or 2.30pm will give you plenty of time at the Skyrail stops. Bring a camera and binoculars, wear comfortable shoes, and for reasons you'll discover later, a bright red, pink or white shirt or blouse if you have one.

Don't be put off by anything but continuous heavy rain, because the rainforest can be at its most fascinating when shrouded in mist – and rainfall increases the number and the spectacle of the waterfalls. The journeys in both directions are as enjoyable as the destination. Outwards you will be travelling in 100-year-old railway carriages, which are carefully maintained and refurbished by Queensland Rail, on the **Kuranda Scenic Railway** (freecall: 1800 620 324; www.ksr.qr.com.au).

When you book, ask for a seat about mid-train (it gets quite noisy at the front) or opt for the Royale Service, where for a little more money, you'll enjoy a refreshing glass of bucks fizz, a fancy name for champagne and orange juice, and a personal guide. Note: there are open-air verandas at each end of some cars for close-to-nature viewing.

A Scenic Ride

The train trundles to Freshwater to pick up more passengers, then continues through the sugar cane fields around Redlynch on Cairns' outer fringe before it climbs up the side of the steep mountain range overlooking the **Barron River Gorge**. The wheels squeal as the track winds into the gullies and around the ridges, with no fewer than 15 tunnels along the way.

A commentary on the railway's construction reminds you of the immensity of the engineering task faced by the predominantly Irish and Italian workforce, who hacked the trackbed out of solid rock with hand tools, buckets and bare hands, aided in the toughest places by dynamite.

The train slows down as it crosses **Stony Creek bridge** over a steep gully, with a backdrop of one of the region's most spectacular waterfalls. Here, pause to think about the obstacles faced by the construction workers – heavy rain that

Left: Barron Falls becomes a trickle in the dry season

caused flooding and landslides, and appalling conditions spreading disease in the base camps. At least 23 workers died before the railway opened up the rich Atherton Tablelands to agriculture and later to tourism. At a brief photo stop at the station overlooking **Barron Falls**, see the river plunge (or trickle, depending on the time of year) from its placid Kuranda reaches and into the gorge.

Kuranda Markets

At the **Kuranda Railway Station**, which you'll reach after 10am, there's a free bus to the village – don't think about walking because it's uphill and you'll cover the same ground walking back to the Skyrail terminal. Most of the village's attractions are attuned to the rail schedules and open from 10am to 4pm, so individual hours will only be included where they differ.

Kuranda village is less than 1km (½ mile) from end to end. It was 'discovered' in the 1960s by hippies who wanted to live in idyllic surroundings, well away from streamlined civilisation, where the occasional recreational smoke (and cultivating the necessary foliage) wouldn't raise an eyebrow. In the 1980s, a sternly disapproving Queensland government took strong action against several North Queensland alternative lifestyle colonies, and one alleged illicit horticulturalist was actually shot while fleeing a dawn raid.

The rainforest setting also attracted a colony of talented artists and craftspeople. The 'original' **Kuranda Markets** (Sun, Wed, Thur and Fri 9am–3pm; tel: 07 4093 7639) sell a cheerful jumble of local and imported crafts and produce, while diagonally across the road at the more commercial **Heritage Markets** (daily 9am–3pm; tel: 07 4093 8060), a range of mostly local craft work is offered. Just outside, you'll see a 'crashed' airliner – a vintage DC-3 formerly used as a film prop – swathed in jungle vegetation.

Above: bustling scene, Kuranda Markets
Left: indigenous kookaburra at Birdworld Kuranda

itineraries

Birds and Butterflies

At the rear of the market a red-tailed black cockatoo or a pink and grey galah stand sentinel outside **Birdworld Kuranda** (daily 9am–4pm; tel: 07 4093 9188; www.birdworld.com). You can step into the enclosure and stroll among over 500 free-flying birds of 55 native and 24 exotic species, including the cassowary, an endangered denizen of North Queensland's rainforests. The birds are tame and friendly, and it's quite common to have a colourful Eclectus parrot or one of its fellow inmates land on your shoulder during the half-hour or more you're likely to spend there. Stay motionless and they're more likely to come to you.

Close by, the **Australian Butterfly Sanctuary** (daily 9.45am–4pm; tel: 07 4093 7575; www.australianbutterflies.com) is home to about 2,000 of these enchanting creatures, with nearly a dozen native species fluttering among the foliage. It's an all-weather attraction, being under cover. The butterflies are reared in the sanctuary, not taken from the wild, so they are not the least bit timid – and if you took my early advice and wore something bright red, pink or white, they are more likely to land on you for a closer inspection. The two prettiest butterflies are the dazzling blue and black Ulysses (attracted to pink, the colour of its favourite flower) and the golden green Cairns Birdwing.

Aim to have lunch after 12.30pm, when the coach tour crowd will have moved on. Kuranda isn't short of places to eat and the competition is reflected in both choice and quality. Australia's well-known propensity for meat pies is nowhere better represented than at **Annabel's Bakery** (Therwine Street; daily 8am–3.30pm; tel: 07 4093 7605) – kangaroo pie is recommended for those who never watched *Skippy* on TV. Nearby, the **Red Ice Cream Cart** is attended by an entertaining multilinguist who sells wonderful ice cream with tropical fruit flavours. Alternatively semi-alfresco **Frogs Restaurant** (11 Coondoo Street; tel: 07 4093 7405): sit at the rear where there's usually a breeze. Order grilled barramundi, and you'll get a free glass of wine or a 'stubbie'. It's all downhill now through Kuranda's very commercialised but still creative main street. Among the landmarks you'll pass en route to the Skyrail are two pubs, known unimaginatively as the **Top Pub** and the **Bottom Pub** – or maybe you won't just pass them if you have worked up a thirst.

Skyrail through the Rainforest

You will have a pre-booked time to arrive at the **Skyrail Rainforest Cableway** (tel: 07 4038 1555; www.skyrail.com.au) for the return trip. Each Skyrail gondola has a sweeping 360-degree view and the full complement of six passengers is not unduly limiting (outside the highest season, you'll normally have only a short wait to get one to yourselves). As you set off, skimming across the Barron River, you see Kuranda and its surrounding rainforest from another perspective. Then you are within a few metres of the rainforest canopy, where you can see the multiple layers that make up its complex ecosystems,

Right: sweep across the rainforest canopy on the Skyrail

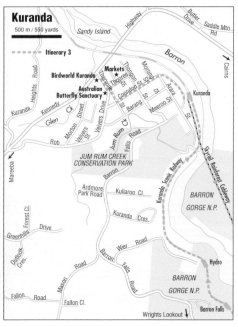

and every so often the breathtaking sight of a placid little stream unsuspectingly meandering towards a sudden cascade into the gorge. The interpretive leaflet that you are given on embarkation (available in 10 languages), identifies the botanical features by reference to the tower numbers.

Boardwalk Lookouts

In about 10 minutes you're at the **Barron Falls** station, where you disembark onto a boardwalk that takes you to two lookouts commanding unforgettable forest-framed views of the falls, especially impressive when the Barron is in full flood.

Here, the efficient **Rainforest Interpretive Centre** has also provided high-tech interactive displays, videos and useful information. Skyrail's next leg sweeps you over more rainforest to **Red Peak**, where you transfer onto a second cableway – the distance being too great for a single cable. At this stop, take advantage of the complimentary ranger-guided walks (every 20 minutes) on walkways just above the forest floor. Back at the Skyrail terminal in Cairns, a low-cost coach will take you back to the railway station to pick up your car, or to your Cairns hotel.

4. TJAPUKAI, PALM COVE AND CAIRNS TROPICAL ZOO
(see pull-out map)

A day that combines a look at Aboriginal art and culture, a bit of lazing on the beach and some exciting wildlife experiences at a tropical zoo.

Although the Tjapukai is right next to the Skyrail terminal in Cairns, I've elected not to combine this attraction with Itinerary 3 as it's too much to do in a single day. Try and get to Tjapukai by 9am. If you're travelling down from a base further north, take the Captain Cook Highway to Smithfield, then follow the signs for Skyrail. Bring swimwear and sun protection for the beach.

At the **Tjapukai Aboriginal Cultural Park** (daily 9am–5pm; tel: 07 4042 9999; www.tjapukai.com.au), the 'story of the Tjapukai people' uses new technology to tell the ancient story of the local Aborigines preserving and presenting their traditional culture. Headset commentaries in eight languages are available in two of the five theatres. The park re-opens at 7pm for dinner and an interactive three-act show four times a week (Tue, Thu, Fri and Sun).

All the plants in the 25-ha (57-acre) site are native to the area, some of which provided the traditional food of the Aborigines. As well as the high-tech exhibits, there are tech-free demonstrations, including instruction in boomerang and spear throwing, how to light a fire without matches and to play the didgeridoo, the traditional wind instrument of the Aborigines. You can also watch a bush medicine show, and there is a restaurant offering specialities like emu burgers and crocodile hot dogs. However, it's too early for lunch, as by about 11am you'll be heading north up the Captain Cook Highway towards Palm Cove.

You might want to make a short detour first, turning west at the first roundabout north of Smithfield, to visit the **A J Hackett Bungy Jumping** tower and watch enthusiasts hurl themselves from the 50-m (164-ft) tower.

Palm Cove Beach
Otherwise, head north on the Captain Cook Highway for about 15 minutes towards Palm Cove, stopping off at Cairns Tropical Zoo on the way to pick up their leaflet detailing the programme of afternoon events – study this at your leisure on the beach and make plans for later.

Palm Cove, the largest of the northern beach resort areas before Port Douglas, is where many visitors base themselves. Unlike Cairns, it has a beach and a nice one too, with waters that are deeper than at other beaches further south, making it clearer in choppy weather. You can rent a catamaran here as long as the wind's below 13 knots, or try your hand at windsurfing.

If you just want to relax on the sands and you like seclusion, take a walk along the very long beach until you get beyond the halfway point, where there are few buildings (you may also notice some relaxation of beachwear formality). If you keep walking it becomes populated again at **Clifton Beach**. Palm Cove also has a deep water jetty, where you'll usually find dozens

Left: Kuranda sightseers taking a break
Above: an Aborigine blowing his didgeridoo at Tjapukai Cultural Park

of locals and visitors trying to prove they're smarter than the fish; the measure of their success is to be found in their plastic buckets – which are often empty.

When you're ready for lunch, enjoy an alfresco meal overlooking the beach at **Far Horizons** (Angsana Resort & Spa, 1 Veivers Road, tel: 07 4055 3000). The menu is rich in local seafood and produce from the market gardens of the Atherton Tablelands. Or spoil yourself at the **Reef House Restaurant** at the luxury Sebel Reef House hotel (99 Williams Esplanade; tel: 07 4055 3633), where subtle Asian flavours enhance the seafood, beef and chicken, and you have superb beach or pool views.

Tropical Zoo

When you've reached your suntan tolerance, retrace your route to the Captain Cook Highway, where

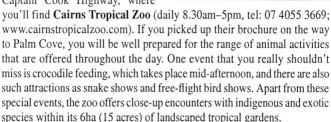

you'll find **Cairns Tropical Zoo** (daily 8.30am–5pm, tel: 07 4055 3669; www.cairnstropicalzoo.com). If you picked up their brochure on the way to Palm Cove, you will be well prepared for the range of animal activities that are offered throughout the day. One event that you really shouldn't miss is crocodile feeding, which takes place mid-afternoon, and there are also such attractions as snake shows and free-flight bird shows. Apart from these special events, the zoo offers close-up encounters with indigenous and exotic species within its 6ha (15 acres) of landscaped tropical gardens.

After this, head back down to Cairns for the evening. Even if you are based further north, it's not far, and it'll round off your day nicely. You can stroll around the Esplanade's **Night Markets** (daily 4.30–11pm), maybe choose a pearl right out of the oyster *(see Shopping, page 77)* and get an inexpensive meal from one of the 14 international outlets within the market. For a more upmarket dinner, you can get a discount at one of three restaurants on the Esplanade as long as you're seated by 6.45pm – choose between

Australian-style seafood at the **Raw Prawn** (103 The Esplanade; tel: 07 4031 5400), Chinese at **Café China** (Rydges Plaza Complex, corner of Spence Street and Grafton Street, tel: 07 4441 2828) and Italian cuisine at **Villa Romano Trattoria** (corner of Esplanade and Aplin Street; tel: 07 4051 9000).

Above: Palm Cove jetty
Left: crocodiles at Cairns Tropical Zoo

5. NORTHERN TABLELAND *(see map, p36)*

A day exploring the bush and agricultural land of the interior, covering a national park, the bush town of Mareeba and quaint Yungaburra village, with wine, coffee and peanuts to taste along the way.

You may prefer a four-wheel-drive vehicle for this trip as there could be some driving over unsealed roads. Wherever you're staying, the Smithfield roundabout, 13km (8 miles) north of Cairns on the Captain Cook Highway, is your starting point for today, where you take the Kennedy Highway towards Kuranda. If you want to link this with Itinerary 6 to make it an overnight trip, book accommodation in the Yungaburra area. Take swimming gear for a dip in the lake.

A few hundred metres after you turn off at the Smithfield roundabout, the road begins its climb up the **Kuranda Range**. It's well made but winding (use second gear), and it requires the driver's full attention. The highway climbs through dense tropical rainforest, and 8km (5 miles) from the roundabout there's a scenic lookout on the right. As the road reaches the top of the range, 660m (2,165ft) above sea level, there are glimpses of the rich rainforest.

Soon you'll cross the **Barron River bridge** and the outskirts of Kuranda, but we won't linger here today because it's already featured in Itinerary 3 *(see page 29)*. Also ignore the Kuranda turn-off, and after a few kilometres you'll notice the vegetation suddenly change from rainforest to dry sclerophyll forest or, as the Australians call it, 'dry bush'. The change is brought about by two factors – less rainfall and different soil, and in this part of Queensland it's also characterised by the presence of large, bulbous-shaped termite mounds. This heralds the beginning of the **Atherton Tablelands**, a rich, rolling territory that slopes upwards to the south, much of it cultivated for agriculture.

Davies Creek and Mareeba Town

After crossing Davies Creek, on the left is a road that leads to the **Davies Creek National Park**. The road is unsealed, so drive with caution. In 8km (5 miles) there's a series of small parking areas; the second one gives best access to a stretch of the creek as it winds and falls through a granite gorge. If it's warm, take a quick dip in any of the dozens of rocky ponds in the area.

After about an hour here, head back onto the Kennedy Highway, where the bush soon gives way to open farmland with mango, citrus and avocado orchards. At the rural town of **Mareeba**, 52km (32 miles) from the Smithfield roundabout, the number of four-wheel-drive vehicles and high-clearance pickup trucks (called 'utilities' or 'utes'), laden with saddles, waterbags and camping gear, indicates that this is a centre for the cattle stations to the west – where roads are often impassable to conventional cars. Tobacco, once a major crop in this area, has been replaced by sugar, tea-tree, coffee, mangoes and other tropical fruits. Stop at **Coffee Works** (136 Mason Street; daily 9am–4pm; tel: 07 4092 4101; www.arabicas.com.au), where locally grown coffee is roasted.

Right: north and west of lush Atherton Tablelands, the landscape becomes drier and dotted with termite mounds

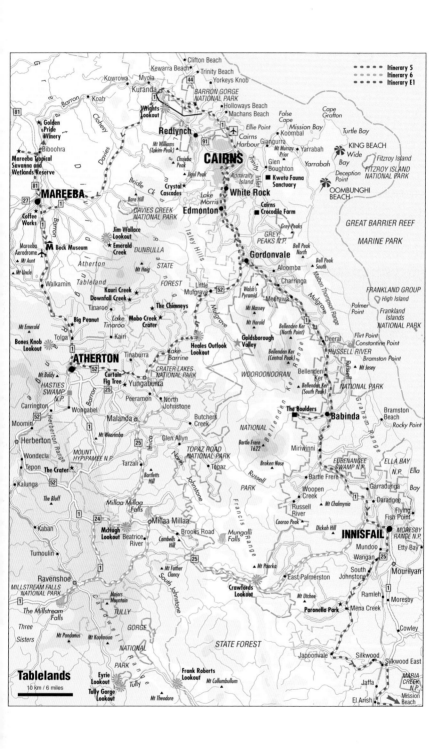

Itinerary 5
Itinerary 6
Itinerary E1

Wine and Wetlands

Drive up the wide main street through Mareeba, and at the approach to Biboohra, 7km (4¼ miles) to the north, a signposted road to the right will take you to the **Golden Pride Winery** (Bilwon Road, daily 8.30am–10pm; tel: 07 4093 2524; www.goldendrop.com). Some 17,500 mango trees here provide the fruit for delicious dry, medium and sweet table wines, ports and liqueurs with a delicate fruity flavour. Not much of the product finds its way to local retailers, so if you like it, buy some before you leave.

Return to the highway and continue north, taking a left turn into Pickford Road at Biboohra. This is another unsealed road, which winds for 7.5km (4½ miles) through sugar cane fields before reaching the **Mareeba Tropical Savanna and Wetland Reserve** (hours are affected by wet season road conditions; www.mareebawetlands.com; tel: 07 4092 3360). Covering over 2,000ha (5,000 acres), this is a gateway to Cape York and the Gulf Savanna Region, presenting a superb introduction to the wonderful biodiversity along the 'Savanna Way' that stretches across the top of Australia from Mareeba to Broome, 3,200km (2,000 miles) away.

Clancy's Lagoon, 121ha (300 acres) of open water, attracts a high concentration of regional wildlife such as brolgas, red-tailed black cockatoos and Australia's only stork, the strikingly elegant Jabiru. The facility is staffed by rangers. You can do several walks on your own, and guided boat tours are available (advance booking required). You can also hire a canoe to paddle around the lakes. Peaceful and contemplative, with lilies floating on the shimmering water, an aviary of rare Gouldian Finches and locally grown tea and coffee at the kiosk, you could easily spend half-a-day here, but limit yourself to an hour because there's so much more to see.

Above: mango wine at Golden Pride
Right: park ranger, Clancy's Lagoon

Historic Aircraft

Heading south out of Mareeba on the Kennedy Highway, if you're into military memorabilia, you could spend an hour or more at two historic aircraft collections. The first, 5km (3 miles) south, is the **Beck Museum** (daily 10am–4pm; tel: 07 4092 3979), where enthusiast Syd Beck is usually on hand to show you around. His extensive collection includes 1940s aircraft, vehicles and weaponry, most of it housed in a huge timber-framed hangar.

Almost opposite is the **Mareeba Aerodrome**, which was constructed in just eight days in March and April 1942 for USAF B17 Flying Fortresses, but was first occupied by the Royal Australian Air Force's 100 Squadron, equipped with Beaufort torpedo bombers. An important link with the region's World War II involvement is the **Rocky Creek Memorial Park**, about 18km (11¼ miles) further on the left, which commemorates the over 100,000 Allied servicemen and women who underwent tropical warfare training there during World War II. A plaque is displayed for each known unit.

Continue down the highway, and look out for the **Big Peanut** on the left as you enter **Tolga** township – hot, freshly roasted peanuts can be sampled here right beside the plantation. On the right just across the railway line, the **Tolga Woodworks Gallery and Café** sells a stunning array of wooden furniture and ornaments – many of which are crafted on the premises.

For lunch, head for the **Homestead Tourist Park** (Beantree Road; tel: 07 4095 4266; reservations required), reached by turning left about 1km (½ mile) south of the town, and continuing for another kilometre. You'll pass through **Tolga Scrub**, a tract of luxuriant rainforest where native cedars and maples grow undisturbed. Australian historic novelist Ion Idriess used to refer to the Atherton Tablelands as 'The Big Scrub' before the term 'rainforest' became fashionable ('Tolga' is the local Aboriginal word for 'Big Scrub').

Above: Beck Museum is for aircraft enthusiasts
Left: Tolga's Big Peanut – you can't miss it

Atherton and Yungaburra

There are other lunch alternatives at Atherton, a few minutes drive south. Turn into Main Street, where two hotels do an inexpensive counter lunch – the restored 1930s **Barron Valley Hotel** at 53 Main Street (tel: 07 4091 1222) and the **Grand Hotel** (tel: 07 4091 4899), an elegant old pub in North Queensland style. If you like gemstones, call in at **Fascinating Facets** at 69 Main Street (Mon–Fri 8.30am–5.00pm; Sat 8.30am–4pm; Sun 10am–4pm; tel: 07 4091 2365; www.crystalcaves.com.au), where a fine display of natural crystals and fossils is set out in a simulated 'cave'.

From Atherton, follow the signs for Malanda and Herberton, then take a left turn where the signpost indicates that it's 12km (7½ miles) to **Yungaburra**. This is where you'll stay if you've elected to combine this and the Itinerary 6 into a two-day trip *(see Accommodation, page 95)*.

As you approach Yungaburra, follow the sign to the **Curtain Fig Tree**. Here, a boardwalk and interpretive display explain how this amazing natural sculpture was formed. First, a draped curtain of aerial roots grew from the parasitic fig as it 'strangled' the host tree, and then the whole thing fell sideways and the fig lowered its roots to the ground.

Continue into Yungaburra, a quaint little village which was until fairly recently an outpost of the new civilisation. Have a stroll around, and especially if you have children with you, take them to the **Chalet Rainforest Gallery** (daily 8.30am–5pm; tel: 07 4095 2144), the only place where you can see the enchanting 'Rainforest Folk', fantasy creatures of the imagination created by doll-maker Chris Boston. The wide range of quality crafts on sale here are 98 percent locally made and make for wonderful memorabilias.

Lake Eacham and Gordonvale

Spend the rest of the afternoon at **Lake Eacham**, a volcanic crater lake in the rainforest, off to the right about 3km (2 miles) along the Gordonvale Road. You can swim in the placid water or follow the signposts to the Ranger Station to pick up self-guided walk leaflets. There is a 2.8-km (1¾-mile) circuit around the lake, which is a cassowary habitat, and you're also likely to see scrub turkeys, pale-yellow robins and tooth-billed bower birds (found only in the Wet Tropics), and a range of water birds.

If returning to Cairns, it's 40km (25 miles) to Gordonvale through 17km (10½ miles) of lush World Heritage rainforest. For 19km (12 miles) it's a winding route, and there are two lookouts with views over the valley below. The route from Gordonvale to Cairns takes the Bruce Highway for 23km (14 miles), an easy but sometimes busy road.

If staying overnight, return to Yungaburra, where the top spot for dinner (or lunch) is **Nick's Swiss-Italian Restaurant** (33 Gillies Highway; tel: 07 4095 3330; closed Mon; reservations necessary). Lots of Nick's personal energy goes into your entertainment here; often, when priorities allow it, he whips out his piano accordion to help you enjoy your grilled lamb loin flavoured with brandy garlic butter.

Right: chef Nick also entertains at his restaurant in Yungaburra

6. SOUTHERN TABLELAND *(see map, p36)*

Cruise through the rainforest, then explore pastoral landscapes before visiting some spectacular waterfalls.

This itinerary can be done on its own or as an extension of Itinerary 5 (see pages 35–9). Get to Lake Barrine National Park in time to have breakfast at the Tea House Restaurant and be ready for the first sailing of the Lake Barrine Rainforest Cruise at 10.15am – it's an hour from Cairns, two hours from Port Douglas, 10 minutes from Yungaburra. From points north of Cairns go south on the Captain Cook Highway, then from Cairns continue further south on the Bruce Highway for about 23km (14 miles). Just beyond Gordonvale, turn right onto the Gillies Highway and, in about 34km (21 miles), Lake Barrine is off to the left. If you stayed the night in Yungaburra (see page 39), take the Gillies Highway east for about 9km (5½ miles) and Lake Barrine will be on the right. Bring swimming gear for a dip in a waterfall pool.

Have breakfast at the **Tea House Restaurant** (daily 9am–5pm; tel: 07 4095 3847). While you're waiting for the **Lake Barrine Rainforest Cruise** (details same as restaurant), take a look at the informative display on the forces that shaped this large volcanic crater lake. Take particular note of the plant specimen in a glass case – it's a stinging plant that you will want to avoid. You'll spend nearly an hour on this fascinating cruise around the perimeter of the lake, with an informative wildlife commentary.

   The trip is equally interesting even if it rains, and in the cooler months you're likely to see amethystine pythons, the world's third largest snake (up to 8.5m/28ft long) sunning themselves on branches. Pelicans and other water birds are usually prolific, and you'll see eels, tortoises and fish in the calm waters. You'll be on the road by 11.30am, unless you decide to walk the 6-km (4-mile) Lake Barrine circuit path (which will take two hours more). A shorter 150-m (500-ft) walk from the Teahouse will take you to the giant twin Kauri pines, estimated to be 1,000 years old.

Tablelands Villages and Pastures

Back on the Gillies Highway, go west and continue through the Tablelands villages of Malanda and Tarzali, amid lush green hillside pastures with fertile red volcanic soil. The black and white Friesian cows grazing in these pastures each produce up to 30 litres (6½ gallons) of milk a day. The **Malanda Dairy Centre** (tel: 07 4095 1234) runs informative tours (Mon–Fri 9am–1pm on the hour).

Go through Tarzali and after 7km (4¼ miles), turn right onto the Ravenshoe Road (don't go into Millaa Millaa yet), and follow the signs to the **McHugh Lookout**. From this vantage point you have sweeping views over the Atherton Tablelands towards Queensland's two highest mountains – **Mount Bellenden Ker** at 1,593m (5,225ft) and the 1,622-m (5,322-ft) **Mount Bartle Frere**. Continue to a T-junction, about 10 minutes' drive further on, and turn left onto the Kennedy Highway, following the signs to Ravenshoe (pronounced 'raven's hoe').

After you've passed through a magnificent natural avenue of tall, elegant white Rose Gums with the apt botanical title of *Eucalyptus Grandis*, the **Windy Hill Wind Farm** is sure to catch your eye, with the giant 22-m (72-ft) long blades of 20 graceful three-bladed windmills swishing musically in the breeze. Each tower stands about 43m (140ft) high, and they generate enough electricity to supply about 3,500 homes, preventing the possible release into the atmosphere of 25,000 tonnes of carbon dioxide that are produced by conventional methods of power generation per year.

High-Altitude Ravenshoe

In another 5km (3 miles), you'll reach **Ravenshoe** (population about 2,000), set up in the 1880s at the top of the Great Dividing Range, 920m (3,000ft) above sea level as a centre for the timber and agriculture industries. At the **Koombooloomba Visitors Centre** (Moore Street; tel: 07 4097 7700), on the right as you enter the town, pick up an information leaflet on the windmills, and a district map with a list of nearby waterfalls in tropical surroundings; try and visit at least one of them.

It's now lunch time and you can absorb Ravenshoe's small town charm while you lunch alfresco at the **Popular Café** at 66 Grigg Street. After lunch check out some of 'Queensland's highests': the **Hotel Tully Falls** reckons it's the highest hotel; there's also the highest bakery; and at the top of the street is the highest pub. Opposite the pub, the attractive **Win's Gallery** relies not on altitude but on solitude, depicted atmospherically by artist-in-residence, Winsome Broad.

Left: Lake Barrine's Teahouse Restaurant. **Above:** cows at a pasture near Malanda. **Right:** signage at Ravenshoe

Gorges and Waterfalls

Some 4.5km (3 miles) out of town, at the end of an unsealed road off the Mount Garnet Road, is **Millstream Falls**, while **Little Millstream Falls** is 2km (1¼ miles) out of town on another (sealed) road, and is actually not so little. A fairly steep five-minute walk down into the gorge rewards you with some memorable tropical scenery. Here in this sheltered chasm the mist and vapour from the waterfalls provides a permanent greenhouse atmosphere.

Retrace your route back to the turning on the right that is signposted 'Millaa Millaa 29km' and follow this road for 2.5 km (1½ miles) until another sign directs you to the 'Scenic Route' (24 km/15 miles to Millaa Millaa). This narrower sealed road winds through lovely farmland and virgin rainforest until you arrive in Millaa Millaa. Just beyond the township turn left to the **Millaa Millaa Falls**, probably the most photographed of the lot.

If you need a snack, stop at the **Falls Teahouse** (daily except Thur 10am–5pm) at the turnoff. Just off the road, the falls descend rather noisily into a large pool. There's parking facilities, toilets and changing rooms, and you can swim across to the waterfall, sit on the rocks and let the cold, falling water pummel you as you ponder that popular Australian expression: 'I wouldn't be dead for quids'.

Homeward bound, take the Palmerston Highway towards Innisfail, then in 5km (3 miles) turn left near the 'steep descent' sign, where there's a Brooks Road sign on the left. This short rural loop road takes you through the hills and valleys past the **Mungalli Creek Dairy**, with its local-produce 'Farmhouse Cheesery' and the **Mungalli**

Above: picturesque Millaa Millaa Falls
Left: explore trails and creeks near Millaa Millaa

Falls Tourist Centre (daily 9am–5pm; tel: 07 4097 2358; www.mungalli falls.com). It's also the site of a 'student village', so you may observe a few intrepid youngsters abseiling down the cliff face. Horse riding is available by appointment, there are some picturesque swimming pools in the creek, and if you're staying longer in the area, there are also nocturnal glow-worm tours.

The Scenic Road Home

You will come back to the sweeping Palmerston Highway, which descends through 14km (8¾ miles) of lush World Heritage rainforest. Along the way there are signs to several attractive rest areas and a campsite at **Henrietta Creek**, and some have walking trails to even more waterfalls. At **Crawford's Lookout** there are views through a clearing down to the North Johnstone River, where you may see some white water rafters testing their skills.

Further along, the road descends until you see a huge banana plantation on the left and the **Nucifora Tea Plantation** on the right. You could stop for some fresh fruit at one of the roadside stalls – usually unmanned, with an 'honesty box' and a set of scales. On this stretch of road, watch out for sugar cane trains during the harvesting season.

Approaching Innisfail, which you'll see in the distance, you'll reach a road junction where there is an avenue of stately Royal Palms. Turn left onto the Bruce Highway (which is busier than the back roads), and the 1¼-hour drive to Cairns is on 84km (52 miles) of mostly excellent road. The sun goes down behind the large twin mountains, and there isn't much twilight in the tropics, so you'll probably arrive in Cairns close to, or just after, dark.

7. CAPE TRIBULATION *(see map, p44)*

Go crocodile-spotting on a river cruise, spend time in the rainforest at the excellent Environmental Centre, then take a quick beach break before heading out to Cape Tribulation.

Your starting time today is set by the need to be at the Daintree River by 9.15am for a 9.30am departure – it's 1¾ hours from Cairns; 40 minutes from Port Douglas. Book ahead for either of the one-hour river cruises (River Train, tel: 07 4090 7676; Bruce Belcher's, tel: 07 4098 7717). There's scope for a little mixing and matching in this itinerary, in case you want to stay longer at one attraction and forego another; or even stay overnight in the Cape Tribulation area. Bring swimming gear and binoculars.

If you're based anywhere between Cairns and Palm Cove, make sure that you set out early enough (6.30am from Cairns) to allow time for breakfast-with-a-view at the **Ellis Beach Bar and Grill** (daily 7am–8pm or later, tel: 07 4055 3534), about 30km (18½ miles) north of Cairns on the left.

Above: fresh fruit from a roadside stall, Palmerston Highway

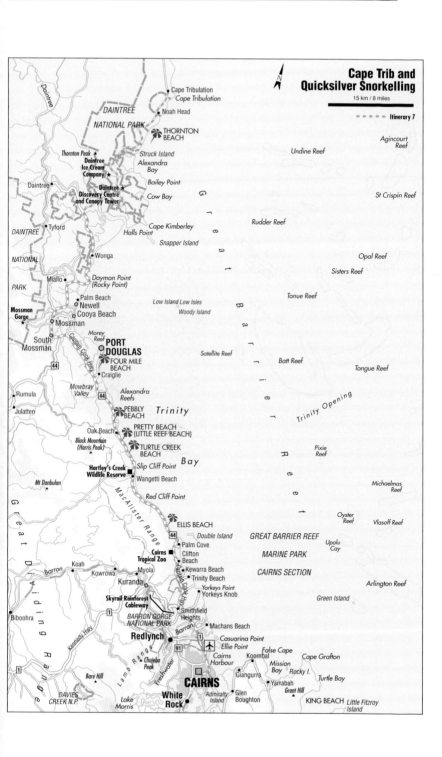

Cape Trib and
Quicksilver Snorkelling

15 km / 8 miles

••••• Itinerary 7

Go north on Captain Cook Highway, and 10km (6 miles) beyond the turnoff to Port Douglas you'll reach **Mossman** *(see Itinerary 2, page 26).* Drive through the small town, heading for the Daintree River ferry crossing. At Miallo there's a slightly confusing Y-junction – take the right fork, which leads to the ferry crossing. If you're booked on the **River Train** (tel: 07 4090 7676; email: reservations@daintreerivertrain.com), a quaint string of small 'carriages' that snakes its way through even the narrowest reaches of the river, follow the signage: the left lane is for the ferry, and the right takes you to the River Train car park.

The other operator is **Bruce Belcher's Daintree River Cruises** (daily 9.30am–4pm; tel 07 4098 7717; www.daintreerivercruises.com.au), a more conventional craft with equally good views for crocodile spotting (binoculars provided), 3km (2 miles) beyond the ferry turnoff on the road to Daintree Village. Both give excellent commentaries on the river's ecosystems and wildlife.

The tours take you up- or downstream, depending on weather and tide factors, through narrow reaches lined with mangroves or rainforests that are rich in wildlife. It's unusual not to spot a crocodile from a safe distance, especially in the cooler months when the huge reptiles come out of the water to sun themselves on the river banks. When crocodiles are spotted, the boat's motors are shut down for a while and you drift in peaceful silence.

Daintree Discovery Centre

By about 10.45am you're back and on board the car ferry for the brief river crossing. On the other side is a good sealed road (watch out for cassowaries, large flightless birds which pose a hazard for motorists as they suddenly dash across the road) and you'll be headed north again, through rainforest and farmland. After 8km (5 miles)

Above: family of cyclists heading for Daintree
Right: view from Alexandra Range Lookout

you'll be at the **Alexandra Range Lookout**, with sweeping views back to the south, across the wide mouth of the Daintree River, Snapper Island and the sugar cane fields and ranges beyond. The road beyond here is well made but narrow and winding, and it requires the driver's full attention.

Some 2km (1¼ miles) from the lookout turn right into Tulip Oak Road for the **Daintree Discovery Centre** (daily 8.30am–5pm; tel: 07 4098 9171; www.daintree-rec.com.au), a world-class interpretive centre that is privately owned, but affiliated to the Wet Tropics Management Authority. It provides a self-guided rainforest booklet and ample interpretive material, including a display centre and two theatres, all giving an excellent insight into what you will see here, from the low-impact boardwalk and the breathtaking heights of the tree-top **Canopy Tower**. At 23m (76ft) high, and with five large viewing platforms at different levels, the tower provides a marvellous experience for photographers, botany enthusiasts and bird watchers – and you can almost feel the trees around you exuding oxygen. There are also audio

guided tours and a 'bush tucker trail'. Many visitors spend hours here, and, because it offers much more than just a quick rainforest fix, you can have your booklet stamped for a repeat visit any time.

A Break at the Beach

A little further on is a sign on the left for the **Ice Cream Company** (daily noon–5pm; tel: 07 4098 9114), which produces ice cream

Above: a close-up of the rainforest
Left: Coconut Beach Resort

flavoured with locally grown tropical fruits in season. They are all worth savouring – coconut, mango, wattleseed, jackfruit and black sapote. If it's too close to lunchtime, you can return here on your way back later in the day. The next thing likely to attract your attention is the **Daintree Tea Plantation** (not open to the public), its neatly-trimmed bushes resembling rows and rows of hedges.

The road remains inland, winding through rich rainforest and farmland until you reach **Thornton Beach**, where there is ample parking and a beautiful uncrowded tract of beach for a quick swim or a laze in the sun. The next 8km (5 miles) of winding road has some truly brutal speed bumps to slow you down, then on the right you'll see the car park for the **Coconut Beach Rainforest Lodge** (tel: 07 4098 0033; www.voyagers.com.au) which is recommended for lunch (10am–3pm). There's a boardwalk over the pandanus swamp to the elegant timber **Cape Restaurant and Bar**, right on the beach, where the bar and stools are made from large chunks of rainforest timbers. You can sit by the pool or inside, and choose from the à la carte menu. Lunch guests can use the pool, or walk down to the beach.

To the Cape

When you've had enough lazing around, you haven't far to go. Less than 1km (½ mile) up the road the sign reads **Cape Tribulation North**, the northern side of the Cape which protrudes at right angles from the main coastline. You will also see 'Kulki' on the signs, which is the traditional aboriginal name for this visitor magnet. Turn right here into the parking area (with picnic tables and toilets), which has a 400-m (¼-mile) boardwalk to an elevated viewing platform. It can be congested here, so if you are not determined to see the actual headland, you might want to stay on at nearby Coconut Beach instead.

From the parking area there's also a short signposted walk over the saddle west of the headland to **Myall Beach**. Don't be alarmed by the goannas (large lizards) which hang out here scavenging the crumbs from the picnickers' tables. The Cape is not without its hostile inhabitants: the beaches have signs warning of stinging box jellyfish which are prevalent from October to May (vinegar is provided near beach entrances for quick treatment), and you are advised not to swim in or near river estuaries, home of saltwater crocodiles; even cassowaries can attack, though it's more likely that they'll avoid you.

From here on, the road is unsealed and suitable only for high-clearance four-wheel-drive vehicles, so returning the way you came is the only option. **Mount Sorrow** and **Thornton's Peak** loom on the right, their peaks often shrouded in mist. The drive back to Cairns will take about two hours (and traffic can be heavy). Between Miallo and Mossman, detour right into Scomazzon Road for **Scomazzons Roadside Stall**, where you can buy locally-grown fruit, including pineapples, strawberry papaw (papaya) and pink grapefruit.

MARINE STINGERS
ARE PRESENT
IN THESE WATERS
DURING THE
SUMMER MONTHS

Right: be careful where you swim in the summer

8. QUICKSILVER SNORKELLING *(see map, p44)*

A fun day trip to the outer Great Barrier Reef, with diving and snorkelling tuition for first-timers, and dry exploring in a semi-submersible boat for non-swimmers.

Several operators do such trips (see page 74) but Port Douglas-based Quicksilver, the most expensive outfit, is also the best. Call Quicksilver in advance (tel: 07 4087 2100; www.quicksilver-cruises.com) to book the trip. You can arrange a coach pickup when you book, and you have the option of joining the vessel at Cairns' Reef Fleet Terminal (departs 8am), Palm Cove Jetty (departs 8.35am) or Port Douglas (departs 10am). Prices start from AU$180 per person. Bring swimming gear and sun protection. There's also a purpose-designed chair-lift to help wheelchair-bound visitors into the water.

Winner of many tourism awards, Quicksilver is well known for its attention to safety and friendliness. Its **Wavepiercer** is a high-speed Cairns-built catamaran with a shallow draft that is eminently suitable for reef operations. Its specially designed hulls literally pierce the waves to eliminate pitching. If you boarded the *Wavepiercer* from either Cairns or Palm Cove, sit back and enjoy the coastal scenery to Port Douglas. After the final pick-up of passengers at Port Douglas, you head for the outer reef. While underway, visit the bow and watch the wavepiercing action of the hulls, sometimes with fun-loving dolphins matching the catamaran's speed.

Before arrival at the huge two-storey floating pontoon, 39 nautical miles offshore, you will be briefed on its many attractions and how best to enjoy them. Quicksilver's deep

Above: snorkellers at Agincourt Reef
Left: creative sun protection

commitment to environmental responsibility becomes readily apparent – the company employs 10 marine biologists. **Agincourt Reef**, where you are heading, is particularly rich in marine life because it's right at the edge of Australia's continental shelf. Beyond it the seabed drops away to a depth of 500m (1,640ft), so the waters lapping the reef have different characteristics from those on the landward side.

Many are content to just snorkel, but even if you have no previous underwater experience, you can have an 'escorted dive' with an instructor literally holding your hand. It's not a dive course and you won't get a certificate, but it can count towards Quicksilver's full four- or five-day courses, for which you may be inspired to enrol. In the forward cabin you're given a thorough half-hour briefing on the use of the equipment, emergency signals and what to expect, followed by 10 to 20 minutes' familiarisation with the equipment.

Exploring Agincourt Reef

On arrival in the Agincourt Reef area, each instructor takes four people and for 30 to 40 minutes shows them the magnificent creatures of the reef – the fish, corals and giant clams – and you can buy a video of your first underwater adventure. Freshwater showers and changing rooms are provided on the pontoon. Taking the escorted dive will still allow plenty of time to enjoy the rest of the reef experience. Snorkels and masks are provided, along with instruction in their use. The staff will help you get accustomed to breathing underwater before setting out amongst the coral 'bommies' – isolated coral outcrops reaching up from the sandy bottom, which attract hosts of colourful fish. All snorkelling is done in a roped area and supervised by safety staff. Fish feeding, between noon and 1.10pm, attracts a regular following from the deep, and optional extras include 'adventure snorkelling' at a more remote site, in a small group accompanied by a marine biologist.

Even if you don't want to get into the water, there's plenty to enjoy, including an underwater viewing area from which you can watch the divers, and a semi-submersible in which you can tour the coral without getting wet. For an extra charge, you can have a brief helicopter flight over the reef or arrange a scenic helicopter flight back to Port Douglas or Cairns.

If you remain aboard the *Wavepiercer* for the trip home, a well-stocked bar is available to conclude your enjoyable day. Whichever way you decide to return to dry land, at 2.40pm, a blast on the ship's horn is the signal for you to return to the pontoon in preparation for departure.

Right: the *Wavepiercer* docked at its pontoon at Agincourt Reef

Excursions

1. MISSION BEACH AND DUNK ISLAND
(see map p36 and p52)

A two-day journey (or longer, depending on whether you extend your stay at Mission Beach or Dunk Island). Head south to see a rainforest World Heritage Site, a Spanish-style castle and a luxuriant tropical island, with bush walking, swimming, sailing and snorkelling.

Book ahead for accommodation at the Dunk Island Resort (tel: 07 4068 8199; www.poresorts.com); also book for the 4.30pm Water Taxi (tel: 07 4068 8310) to Dunk Island and for the Quick Cat Cruise (tel: 07 4068 7289) if you plan to take up that option. Wherever you're based, you need to set out early – 7.30am from Cairns; earlier if you are further north – taking a packed breakfast. First, make your way to Cairns, then take the Bruce Highway south and follow directions below. Take what you need for an overnight stay, including sturdy walking shoes, swimming gear and sun protection. Depending on the time of year, you might need an umbrella.

Travelling south on the Bruce Highway, you'll pass through Edmonton and Gordonvale; then 23km (14¼ miles) from Cairns, if it's crushing season, you'll see the white plume of smoke from the Mulgrave Sugar Mill. Straight ahead is the aptly-named **Walsh's Pyramid**, a forbidding 922-m (3,025-ft) monolith where the annual 'mountain man race' is held – usually the winner scales it in less than 1½ hours, but 2½ is more realistic if you're tempted.

Rainfall and Rainforest

As you pass through the sugar cane fields, notice the increasing richness of the tropical greenery. You're approaching the Australian mainland's area of highest rainfall, measured not in millimetres but in metres! **Babinda** and nearby **Tully** compete annually for the 'Golden Gumboot Award', which goes to the town recording the highest annual average: usually around 4.6m (over 15ft). The locals (who, even with this record, still tend to exaggerate) will tell you it rains for 11 months, and drips off the trees for the rest of the year. In actual fact, large amounts of rain tend to fall in a very short time, and there's plenty of tropical sunshine to add its influence to the unusually diverse vegetation.

At Babinda, just after you pass the historic sugar mill, turn right and follow signs to **The Boulders**, a Wet Tropics World Heritage area with a nature reserve and visitor facilities (toilets, picnic tables, well-marked trails). The 850-m (½-mile) **Rainforest Circuit** walk takes you across a suspension bridge and to clear pools where you can cool off amidst massed green foliage, giant tree ferns, moss-covered boulders, coiled and curling vines and tall, ancient trees. A

Left: Mission Beach
Right: intrepid young explorer

second, shorter walk leads to the **Boulders Gorge** past the Devils Pool. The stream rises in the high country between Queensland's two tallest mountains, where rainfall of 600mm (nearly 2ft) has been recorded in a 24-hour period.

Don't even think about swimming here because there have been a number of drownings, especially of young, single men who have slipped on the rocks and been trapped under the surging cascades. There is a legend that they are lured by the singing of the spirit of Oolana, a beautiful young Aboriginal woman who, though betrothed to a respected elder of her own tribe, fell in love with a visitor from a neighbouring tribe. They ran away, but were found here by the waters edge, and as Oolana's tribe were dragging her back she broke away and flung herself into the gentle waters of the creek. Just then a tremendous upheaval occurred – the land shook with terror and sorrow, and rushing water came cascading over the whole area. Huge boulders were thrown up and she disappeared among them. They say that her spirit remains and her anguished cry can sometimes be heard, calling her lover to return.

The Spaniard's Castle

Back in **Babinda**, call in at **Babinda District Arts and Crafts** (13 Munro Street; daily 9am–4pm; tel: 07 4067 2044), which is staffed by volunteers and stocks a diversity of craftwork, including wooden bowls containing hand-crafted 'fruits of the tropical rainforest' – a bright display ranging from the blue quandong fruit to the glossy red fruit of the lacewing vine, perfect replicas of the colourful flashes you may see in the rainforest.

Head south again on the Bruce Highway. The drive to **Innisfail** is a scenic one, with jungle-clad mountains fringing the rich farm-land. Drive through Innisfail and instead of taking the right fork south to Townsville, go straight ahead to **South Johnstone**, with the South Johnstone River on your left – do not swim here, it's the home of the usually hungry *Crocodylus Johnstoni*, which grows to lengths of about 5m (16½ ft). Keeping a lookout for sugar cane trains in season, drive through the banana, papaw, citrus and sugar

Map: Mission Beach and Dunk Island — 5 km / 3 miles

MARIA CREEK NATIONAL PARK
Cassowary Coast
Cairns
Garners Point
Ninney Point
Bingil Bay
CLUMP MOUNTAIN NATIONAL PARK
Bicton Hill
★ Lacey Creek
Clump Point
South Maria Ck
Mission Beach
GREAT BARRIER REEF
MARINE
Luff Hill
MISSION BEACH
PARK
Wongaling Beach
Mt Tim O'Shanter
Beaver Cay Reef
Purtaboi Island
Toogan Toogan Pt
Tully
Pall-Koo-Loo Pt
Dunk Island Resort
Dunk Island
Lugger Bay
Coconut Bay
HULL RIVER NATIONAL PARK
Tam O'Shanter Point
- - - - Itinerary E1

Above: scenic Boulders Gorge

cane farms to **Paronella Park** (daily 9am–9pm; tel: 07 4065 3225; www.paronellapark.com.au). Here, the partially restored ruins of North Queensland's first tourist attraction lie in 5ha (13 acres) of rainforest. It was built by José Paronella, a young Spanish immigrant who fell in love with the region in 1913 and eventually purchased the property and built a home there. He then went on to construct a down-scaled Spanish castle beside the **Mena Creek Falls** and surround it with pleasure gardens which were designed for public enjoyment. The privately-owned fantasy park has won several heritage awards and has been featured in a number of movies and TV shows. You can have a picnic, and swim safely in the falls.

From here, you're about 45 minutes from **Mission Beach**. Follow the signs through even greener rural land to Silkwood (23km/14 miles), and in 3km (2 miles) turn right onto the highway and continue to El Arish. Turn left, and 16km (10 miles) of sometimes winding road takes you to the Mission Beach area – five communities strung out along a coastline of broad white-sand beaches backed by coconut palms and lapped by (usually) crystal-blue water.

You should have some time to spare before your pre-booked place on the 4.30pm water taxi to Dunk Island, so call in at **Mission Beach Tourism** (daily 9am–5pm; tel: 07 4068 7099; www.missionbeachtourism.com) for information, then go next door to the **Environment Centre** (daily 10am–4pm) to watch a 10-minute video on the rare and endangered cassowary, which still exists in notable numbers in the rainforests. If you decide to extend your stay at the Mission Beach area, there is an ample range of hotels to meet all budgets (*see page 96*).

Dunk Island

Take the South Mission Beach Road to the **Water Taxi** (tel: 07 4068 8310) departure point in **Banfield Parade** on Wongaling Beach. Park your car in the open paddock at the rear of the office; and note that you'll be wading out through shallow (warm) water to board the boat – anything below your knees will be getting wet (staff will load your baggage). In 15 minutes you'll be on the jetty at **Dunk Island**, where a resort bus will be waiting to take you to the reception desk to check in. Dunk Island is the self-styled 'Island of Peace and Plenty', a translation of its Aboriginal name, 'Coonanglebah', and the accommodation options range from standard twin-bedded rooms to suites and cabanas.

As the sun sets over the mainland mountains, tiny candles light the stairways and tables and the tropical night comes alive. Try a pre-dinner 'E J Banfield' cocktail, named after the first white settler who famously heard 'the beat of a different drum' and stayed on the island for 25 years, eventually writing his well-known book, *Confessions of a Beachcomber*. You can dine from a bounteous beachside barbecue or à la carte, and there will probably

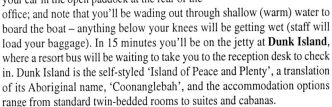

Right: Japanese tourists at the suspension bridge over Mena Creek Falls, Paronella Park

be live entertainment. Dunk Island is particularly good for families, with a babysitting service, child-care provided by the Kids' Club and a teenage club for those up to 16 years offering all kinds of fun. There are plenty of activities included in the price of your accommodation, and you might want to stay for more than one night to take full advantage of them. The resort also provides maps of the bushwalking tracks and lists of the interesting birdlife you might be able to identify along the way.

You should also set aside some time to walk (40 minutes) to the **Bruce Arthur's Artists' Colony** (Thur–Sun 10am–1pm), an enclave of resident

and visiting artists exhibiting Dunk Island-produced paintings, pottery and jewellery. If you're tempted to purchase something from the display, it will be packed and delivered to your room at the resort. You can then return the way you came, or complete a rainforest circuit track which will take you about another 1½ hours, with some stunning views of the island-studded bay.

Beaver Cay

Among the options at Dunk Island resort is a cruise with **Quick Cat Cruises** (tel: 07 4068 7289; reservations required; departure 10.45am) to **Beaver Cay** reef, 25 nautical miles off the coast. If you're returning to the mainland later on the same day, check out by 11am before you set off, and make arrangements for your baggage to be put aboard the vessel when it calls back at Dunk Island after the reef trip. Would-be divers will see an instructional video during the hour-long voyage

to the cay. The crew will also arrange an introductory dive for children from the age of 12, as long as you can satisfactorily complete their medical questionnaire. However, if you prefer to snorkel, you can do just that.

The voyage includes a trip in a glass-bottomed boat – the large spangled emperor fish underwater make you wonder who's watching whom – and snorkelling equipment is available on board. Beaver Cay has no vegetation, just a few migratory birds walking the soft, pale golden sand. Like a true desert island it's very exposed on a hot day, so put on plenty of sunscreen. Whales are sometimes sighted here during the migratory months of July and August.

The Quick Cat leaves Beaver Cay at about 3.15pm, stopping to pick up passengers who opted out of the cruise (and your luggage) at Dunk at 4.30pm,

arriving on the mainland at **Clump Point** by 5pm. A minibus will drop you back at your car (or hotel, if you are staying on in the Mission Beach area). Then you simply backtrack to the Bruce Highway and head north – it's about two hours to Cairns and three hours to Port Douglas.

Above: diving into Beaver Cay
Right: Dunk Island

2. CRUISING THE CORAL COAST *(see map, p56)*

A four-night cruise that follows the course of Captain Cook's voyage, calling at Fitzroy Island and Cooktown, before heading out to the coral cays and islands of the Great Barrier Reef.

Book well in advance with Captain Cook Cruises (tel: Cairns office 07 4031 4433, or Sydney office 02 9206 1122; www.captaincook.com.au). Berths are frequently sold out, especially during high season. The price (starting at under AU$1,650 at time of press) includes all meals, entertainment and activities. You'll need to bring swimwear and suitable clothing for trips ashore, walking shoes and sun-protection, a camera (preferably with a polarising filter) and binoculars, if you have them. If you want to dive bring your Open Water Dive Certificate. You'll need to be at Cairns by 1pm, for departure at 2pm on Monday; you'll arrive back at 8am on Friday.

The **MV** *Reef Endeavour*, because it is especially designed and equipped for reef cruising, offers rare insights into some of the more remote and unspoiled parts of the Great Barrier Reef. There is also a three-night cruise to the south, but I recommend the northern circuit because it takes you to some locations that are hard to reach any other way. Accommodation is either in staterooms that open onto the outside deck, or cabins that open onto inside passageways (with portholes giving good natural lighting); some have double beds, but most have twin beds and all have en suite bathrooms.

On-board facilities include a swimming pool, sauna, spa and gym, and the relatively small passenger complement (about 150) makes for a friendly atmosphere. Daily information bulletins keep you posted on the ship's itinerary and activities, and safety is carefully observed – everyone is counted off and back on to the vessel at every stop.

Above: the MV *Reef Endeavour* is perfect for exploring the Great Barrier Reef

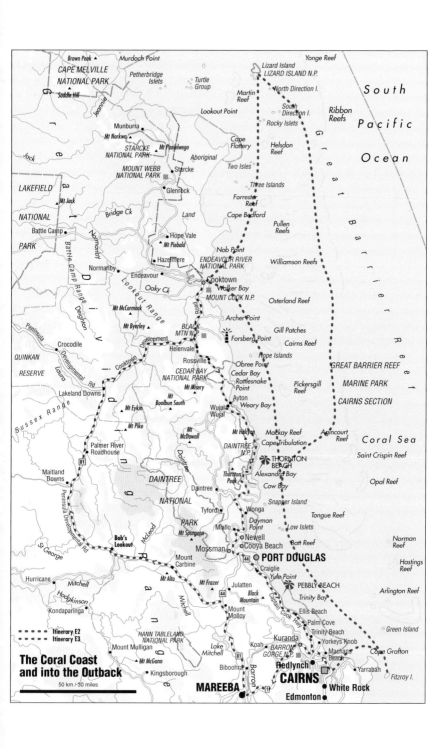

The Coral Coast
and into the Outback

50 km / 30 miles

Itinerary E2
Itinerary E3

excursions

Day One – Monday

The first afternoon sees you sailing northeast down Trinity Inlet, past the granite faces of False Cape and Cape Grafton, to anchor off **Fitzroy Island** by 4pm. This rainforested mountain juts from the sea, much of it fringed by coral, and you are taken ashore on shuttle boats (try to get on the first one). You're ashore for two hours, with plenty of time (weather permitting) for a hike to the lighthouse, atop the island's highest peak. The 1½-hour walk is reasonably easy and well-marked, and takes you through tracts of magnificent rainforest with glimpses of the sea. If you're staying on the beach, you still need to wear shoes because it's not sand, but crushed coral. The last boat returns to the ship at 6pm, in time for dinner at 7.30. Dinners on board are à la carte; breakfasts and lunches are buffet style with plenty of choice and an emphasis on tropical fruit and regional produce.

As your voyage unfolds you can follow your progress in the Chart House Lounge, right at the top of the ship. Much of the first night's voyage closely resembles the route followed by Captain James Cook, who first discovered and charted most of Australia's east coast *(see page 11)*. The charts will show you the hundreds of reefs and shoals dotted between the mainland and the outer Barrier Reef. Cook was an extremely precise navigator, but without charts he had to rely on a masthead lookout. Tonight, guided by detailed charts, beacons and satellite navigation, you'll be passing close to the point where, for Cook, that lookout was not enough.

Day Two – Tuesday

Your Tuesday itinerary starts with a trip ashore to visit **Cooktown** *(see also page 61)* where an optional commentated minibus tour (for a small additional fee) ensures you'll take in as much as possible on this brief visit. If you don't avail yourself of the bus tour, head straight for the **James Cook Museum** *(see page 61)*, which encapsulates most of the town's colourful history. Cook spent 48 days here, but you'll be back aboard at about 11.30am, again closely following his route northwards.

The next stop is at **Two Isles**, the only true coral cay on your itinerary, where you can snorkel and/or take the rewarding 45-minute beach walk right around the island in the company of an experienced biologist. You'll then pass a number of typical coral cays, more numerous in this area than almost anywhere else along the Great Barrier Reef, which are characterised by the low elevation of their richly vegetated sand dunes, the vivid white coral sand of their beaches, and the opalescent colour which the underlying coral imparts to the shallow blue water inside their fringing reefs.

Sailing on, you'll see ahead the towering granite bulk of **Lizard Island** (named by Cook), with its **Blue Lagoon** – a large expanse

Right: sundeck, MV Reef *Endeavour*

of coral-studded shallows inside a fringing reef that joins Lizard with two other islands. Around dusk, you drop anchor in **Watson's Bay**, in the lee of the island, named after an early settler named Mary Watson, who along with her baby and two Chinese servants, perished at sea while fleeing from marauding mainland Aboriginal tribes. Just around the headland is luxurious **Lizard Island Lodge**, a playground for the rich and famous; non-residents are discouraged.

Day Three – Wednesday

The first (optional) attraction is only a good idea if you are fairly fit. Book an early call, put on some durable walking footwear and join a guided pre-breakfast walk up the rocky spine of Lizard Island to **Cook's Look**, at 359m (1,179ft) the island's highest point. Frustrated by what he described as a 'labyrinthe' of coral shoals, Cook ascended the same hill in his quest for a way to open water. He saw the white lines of breakers, similar to those that you will observe crashing onto the reefs, and identified a safe passage through. There are two guides on your walk – a leader and another to take care of anybody who may find the pace too rapid. In that event, you will take a break at a location with a view amidst the diverse native vegetation (including orchids and flowering trees), and wait until the others return. Back on the beach, you're ferried to the ship for a well-earned breakfast.

For the rest of the day, the ship provides shuttles to and from the beach, where you can snorkel in the clear water in a marked-out and patrolled area, enjoy the coral from a glass-bottomed boat, or sunbathe (taking care to protect yourself in this exposed environment). The crew set up a base camp with cool drinks, fresh towels and spare snorkelling equipment. After lunch on the ship, there's a guided walk of about 5km (3 miles) along a relatively flat path to the Blue Lagoon, where you can enjoy the solitude of its lovely beaches and swim in its calm waters. There is, however, no snorkelling here. You return, as usual, to the ship for dinner and evening entertainment.

Day Four – Thursday

Your overnight voyage will have brought you to the **Ribbon Reefs**, where the edge of the Great Barrier Reef is most clearly defined and the deep blue

water beyond attracts the giant black marlin, which millionaire sailors pursue relentlessly (but not always successfully). Ahead are the aqua-coloured shallows of the reef at its best, and across the lagoon you'll clearly see the line of surf beating incessantly on the reef's seaward side. The day is filled with options for diving, snorkelling or glass-bottomed boat viewing at this world-renowned reef site. The best time for snorkelling is at lower tides, when the shallows are better protected and the water is calmer.

On your last evening, the *Reef Endeavour* cruises quietly through the darkness, arriving in Cairns in the early hours and discharging its passengers after breakfast the following day, at about 8am.

Left: trek up to Cook's Look for amazing vistas

3. CAPE YORK PENINSULA *(see map, p56)*

An overnight trip involving a four-wheel-drive exploration of the remote Outback of Cape York Peninsula, including a visit to historic Cooktown and back down the coastal road.

Make an early start and follow the directions in Itinerary 5 (see page 35) to Mareeba, then pick up the route detailed below. You will need an off-road vehicle (Hertz rental formalities include a 20-minute crash course on its use), and make sure no significant rain is forecast, otherwise you have to miss out on the coastal route. The Royal Automobile Club of Queensland or RACQ (tel: 1300 130 595; www.racq.com.au) can provide useful motoring information. Book a room at Cooktown's Milkwood Lodge (tel: 07 4069 5007; www.milkwoodlodge.com), or rent a four-wheel-drive campervan (www.hertzcampervans.com.au) instead. Only informal clothing will be needed, and swimming gear. Take some food and drinks in an 'esky' (insulated cooler); ice is sold at most service stations; these are few and far between in the Outback, so top up with fuel at every opportunity.

On the **Peninsular Development Road** from Mareeba it's 185km (115 miles) to Lakeland Downs, and 266km (165 miles) to Cooktown. Here and there you'll see signs warning of 'road trains' – huge trucks with multiple trailers, which are very heavy and of limited manoeuvrability. If you encounter one on an unsealed road, pull over as far as you can, stop the car and wind up the windows, because they raise a great deal of dust. Having said that, the locals reckon if they can see three at once, it's a traffic jam.

This is where the **Outback** really begins. You're quite suddenly in a wide expanse of under-populated land, some of it cleared for grazing

Above: Outback scenery
Right: typical 'road train'

and some open bush with a great diversity of forest types. Much of the landscape is unfenced, so beware of wandering cattle and kangaroos. The latter are most active in the early morning and at dusk when they sometimes emerge from the bush at high speed, inflicting serious damage on them-

selves and your vehicle. There are rest bays near some of the bridges, and in dry weather the streams that are still running attract lots of bird life. You might also see a platypus swimming low in the waters of a quiet billabong.

At **Mount Molloy**, if the bakery is open, buy something fresh from the oven and drive to the rest area at **Rifle Creek**, about 2km (1¼ miles) beyond the town on the left, with tall, rustling eucalypts providing shade, and have your picnic.

From the road, the coastal ranges on the distant right are rainforested, while the heights on the left are barren rocky outcrops. Food and fuel outlets are limited to the isolated townships along the way, and wide open spaces separate the sparse homesteads, marked only by a dirt driveway and a mailbox. Beyond **Mount Carbine**, once a thriving mining township but now offering little beyond a store, a hotel/motel and a roadhouse, the road sweeps up a steep range to **Bob's Lookout**, with a view of the wilderness that extends to the horizon.

Lakeland Downs and Black Mountain

Some 84km (52 miles) beyond Mount Carbine, the **Palmer River Goldfields Roadhouse** (tel: 07 4060 2152), framed by colourful bougainvillea and lined with local slate, is a good spot to enjoy a snack. You can also browse amongst the small collection of memorabilia from the Palmer River gold rush, which produced 80 tons of gold before the lode was exhausted.

Over and down the mighty Byerstown Range, you reach the open plains of **Lakeland Downs**, with a permanent population of about 100 hardy souls. There were once great plans for this settlement, including a vast irrigation project, land clearance for grain crops and a railway to the coast near Cooktown, but the project ran out of cash and the land was divided into small farms which now grow coffee, navy beans, peanuts, pawpaw and bananas. Locally grown Laura Valley coffee is available from the **Lakeland Coffee House and Store**. If you're ready for lunch, the **Lakeland Downs Hotel** (noon–2.30pm; tel: 07 4060 2142) can oblige.

Here, the unsealed road forks left to Cape York, but continue straight on the winding, mostly gravel, road for the 79km (49 miles) to Cooktown, and take heed of the sign: 'Drive according to prevailing conditions'; it's also a good idea to turn on your headlights because of the clouds of dust your vehicle will stir up. It was along this approximate route, with its diverse landscape playing host to 'vine scrub' which obstructed the early explorers, that the prospectors who survived the Aborigines' vigorous armed resistance to their passage found their way to the goldfields. Just after the sealed road

Above: wandering cattle are one of the road hazards on the Cooktown route

recommences, a causeway and a low bridge take you across the **Annan River Gorge**, where debris in the foliage betrays occasional high flood levels. Three kilometres (2 miles) further on, stop at the lookout which commands a view of the amazing **Black Mountain**, which has the appearance of a huge pile of black boulders. It has found a place in Aboriginal and subsequent European legend, mostly surrounding the supposed mysterious disappearance of climbers who entered its dark caverns. A plaque explains the weird formation, and sometimes white cockatoos can be seen silhouetted against it, circling in the thermals rising from the warm rocks.

Captain Cook's Town

Re-crossing the Annan River, this time close to its mouth, you'll enter **Cooktown** (population 1,500), named after Captain James Cook who beached his exploration ship here in 1770 after damaging it on a coral reef. Four-wheel-drive vehicles dominate the main street – squadrons of visitors, many of them from the southern states, flock to the Cape York Peninsula every winter to pit their vehicles, equipment and driving skills against the rugged terrain and the boneshaking bush tracks.

If you're driving a camper, head for the 3.2-ha (8-acre) **Cooktown Holiday Park** (tel: 07 4069 5417) at the junction of Charlotte Street and McIvor Road. Alternatively, you may already have made a reservation at **Milkwood Lodge** *(see page 59)* in Annan Road.

There should be plenty of time after you've checked in to visit the town's historic centrepiece, the **James Cook Museum** (daily 9.30am–4pm; tel: 07 4069 5386), on the corner of Furneaux Street and Helen Street. Occupying an impressive building, it is now administered by the National Trust of Queensland, and one of its prized exhibits is a

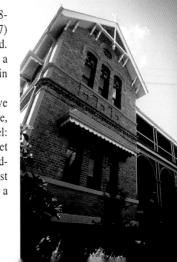

Above: Black Mountain
Right: James Cook Museum

cannon and the anchor from the *Endeavour*, recovered from the reef in 1969.

Cooktown's **Nature's Paradise** in the Botanic Gardens (Walker Street; daily 9am–5pm; tel 07 4069 6004) is also worth a visit. The centre, built of corrugated iron and set in natural bush, features local and travelling exhibitions. If there's time, pause for a drink at **Vera's in the Gardens**, and you can also take a 600-m (⅓-mile) walk through natural bushland to **Finch Bay** – you may see wallabies along the way, and there'll be wild flowers in spring and a profusion of butterflies in summer. The **Cooktown Cemetery** in McIvor Road contains a **Chinese Shrine** honouring the estimated 20,000 Chinese prospectors who worked in the goldfields, many of whom are buried here.

Before dinner, drive (or walk) up **Grassy Hill** with its old lighthouse, and gaze out across the sweep of coastline and maze of coral reefs to seaward, as Cook once did in his search for a safe passage. Watch the sunset, perhaps, and take in a few lungfuls of the clean sea air. Alternatively, if you enjoy fishing you can soak up the evening peace of the jetty. Bait and tackle are available from the **Lure Shop**, at 209 Charlotte Street. As for nightlife – maybe, in 20 or 30 years. Meanwhile, the **Bowling Club** at Charlotte Street (daily 6–9pm; tel: 07 4069 5819) welcomes visitors.

Cedar Bay and the Coast Road

In the morning, leave by about 10.30am if you intend to return to Cairns by nightfall. But first (if you're not already out there fishing) stroll along the **Esplanade** to the wharf and have breakfast at **Cook's Landing Kiosk** (daily from 7am–5pm). On the way, you'll see several monuments, including those honouring Captain Cook and the battling gold miners.

Top up with fuel here, because there's no guarantee of getting any before you reach Cape Tribulation, and load up the 'esky' with supplies and ice if you want a picnic lunch (though there are places to eat along the way). Then retrace yesterday's route to the point just past Black Mountain where a sign directs you left to the **Lions Den** at Helenvale (www.lionsden.com.au). Remember to engage your hubs in four-wheel-drive mode, or you'll discover

your mistake at the least opportune moment! The proudly primitive Lion's Den pub, built in 1875, is an unsophisticated structure, often peopled by local characters watching the four-wheel-drive procession with quizzical amusement. In the

Above: lighthouse on Grassy Hill
Left: Lion's Den pub, Cooktown
Right: view of Bloomfield River

shop at the far end of the pub there are a few souvenirs, including some Aboriginal pieces – a Lion's Den singlet is *de rigueur* for anybody north of the 16th parallel.

From here on there's little in the way of civilisation and the road is mostly formed gravel, some of it corrugated, with a few sealed tracts identifying the proximity of homes whose occupants don't enjoy eating dust. Watch out for oncoming traffic along the narrow sections. The road mostly passes through rainforest, and at **Cedar Bay National Park** (tel: 07 4098 0052 for information) the going gets increasingly rugged. For lunch, stop at the **Weary Bay Café** (known to locals as 'Viv's Place') at 11 West Street Ayton (tel: 07 4060 8266), open for light meals or takeaways (8am–4pm daily).

The Coral Coast Road

When you see the **Bloomfield River** on the left you're approaching the Wujal Wujal Aboriginal community (no visitor facilities) and the road soon takes a sharp left turn across the **Bloomfield Causeway**. But first, go straight ahead to the **Bloomfield Falls** car park where it's just a short walk to the falls. If the causeway is under water (not often but it's tidal), it may still be safe to cross – ask the locals for advice. This newest section of this road is very slippery when wet so drive carefully and give way to vehicles travelling uphill. If you slip off the road, just wait for assistance from one of the frequent four-wheel-drive vehicles that pass this way. Although this is called the **Coral Coast Road**, there are only a couple of places along this stretch where you'll catch a glimpse of the sea through the rainforest.

Some 62km (38½ miles) from the turnoff and 96km (59½ miles) from Cooktown, you'll reach the **Cape Tribulation** section of the **Daintree National Park** *(see Itinerary 7, page 43)* and you're back on sealed roads. You should have time to reach Cairns before it gets dark, unless you decide to stay in the area and follow up on some of the attractions detailed in Itinerary 7.

4. THE WHITSUNDAY ISLANDS *(see map, p66)*

The Whitsunday Islands' crystal-clear waters, their brilliantly white sand beaches with fringing coral reefs, and the charming interface of reef with verdant tropical rainforest, draw visitors from all over the world to popular Airlie Beach and nearby Hamilton Island.

The information here is for visitors from Cairns. If flying from Brisbane, Sydney or Melbourne, just adapt this itinerary as you see fit. Three days is the least possible time you need in the Whitsundays – to justify the travel cost and to savour its attractions. There's plenty to do in the Whitsundays if you stay for a week or longer. You need to decide on a base: either Airlie Beach on the mainland, Hamilton Island (see page 96 for details of both) or any one of the islands in the Whitsundays. Note: this itinerary only advises on options in Airlie Beach or Hamilton. Wherever your base is, buy a return flight direct to Hamilton Island with Sunstate Airlines (book with Qantas, tel: 31313; www.qantas.com.au). If driving from Cairns, the 632-km (393-mile) ride along the Bruce Highway to Airlie Beach will take at least 7 hours. Hamilton Island is connected to Shute Harbour on the mainland by a 30-minute ferry ride, from where Airlie Beach is a 10-minute taxi ride away.

The Whitsunday Group

A collection of 74 islands (or more, depending on what sized rock you would describe as an island) strewn in the aquamarine waters of the Great Barrier Reef make up the gorgeous Whitsunday Islands. Most are uninhabited with numerous bays and beaches to explore, and amazing coral reefs to discover. The islands lie on the same tropical latitude as Honolulu in the northern hemisphere, and enjoy year-round warm tropical temperatures averaging about 27.4 degrees C (81 degrees F).

The Whitsundays are in fact the tips of mountain peaks submerged in water. After the last Ice Age, the melting of the polar ice caps drowned the valleys in between the mountains, creating the network of islands you see today. The waters surrounding the islands are part of the Great Barrier Reef Marine Park.

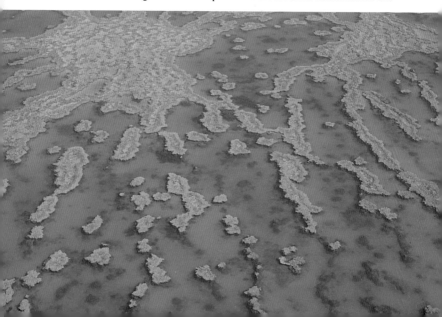

Staying at Hamilton

Hamilton Island (www.hamilton island.com.au) at 750 hectares (1,853 acres) is one of seven islands with resorts – the others are Long, Lindeman, South Molle, Daydream, Hook and Hayman. Hamilton is the only island with its own airport for commercial and charter flights. It is also possible to get to Hamilton Island by sea as it's only 16km (10 miles) southeast of Shute Harbour on the mainland, with six daily Blue Ferry services making the direct trip.

Over 70 per cent of Hamilton has been carefully preserved in its natural state so that visitors can continue to enjoy the pristine beauty of the island's fabulous beaches, unspoilt nature trails and secluded hideaways. Because it was all built in one go, for the purpose of upmarket tourism, Hamilton Island has been described variously as a 'daiquiri Disneyland' or 'a theme park waiting for a theme'. There are several room types spread all over the island, none of which can be termed inexpensive. Choose from the Beach Club, Reef View Hotel, Whitsunday Apartments and the Palm Bungalows and Terrace. The low-rise Palm Terrace is aimed at the 'budget traveller' but even then the rooms are priced from AU$250 a night.

There is plenty to keep you occupied: cruises to the Great Barrier Reef, waterskiing, windsurfing, catamaran and yacht sailing, tennis, game fishing, nature walks, whale watching (mid July to September), scenic flights, safari tours or simply just relaxing by one of the six resort pools.

Exploring Hamilton

The best way to explore Hamilton is to hire an electric 'buggy', the standard vehicle on the island, available by the hour or the half-day from either of two agencies near the marina. These automated little machines have a speed limiter set at 20kmh (12mph), but they can tackle Hamilton's steepest hill. The agency will provide a map, but it's impossible to get lost – though you need to be aware that some of the residential streets aren't marked on the map, probably because they are signposted 'no buggies'. You should park and walk now and then, just to see how the wealthy, who own holiday homes on the island, live.

Be sure to drive up **One Tree Hill**, the highest point on the island, for an overview. On the way back down the hill, take the first left for a glimpse of the island's timber **All Saints Church**. One of Hamilton's lesser-known industries is arranging weddings. Anyone with a willing partner can arrange to get married here, but

Left: aerial view of the coral reef in the Whitsundays. **Above:** lunch at Toucan Tango. **Right:** activity board

you'll need to book ahead because trade can be brisk, especially during the Japanese springtime.

Hamilton's shops and boutiques are worth browsing, but the prices reflect the fact that retailers have to pay high rents to the conglomerate that owns the island.

In the evening, soak up the cosmopolitan atmosphere around the marina village and see which one of the 10 restaurants takes your fancy for dinner. Overlooking the marina is **Spinnaker's Bar and Grill**, a good mid-priced option which serves juicy sizzling steaks cooked any way you like them. If you prefer fine-dining, the **Beach House Restaurant** serves modern Australian cuisine using the best of local produce. For something more casual, the **Toucan Tango Café** is great for families.

Staying at Airlie Beach

Many people choose to stay at **Airlie Beach** on the mainland simply because accommodation here is cheaper and there is a reasonably good selection of restaurants and shops. Some visitors divide their time between Airlie Beach and a stay at one of the island resorts. Unfortunately, Airlie has no real beach, only a narrow strip of sand that becomes a rocky mudflat when the tide is low. To make up for it, a new and sprawling artificial lagoon set in landscaped gardens has been built. Airlie Beach is a 10-minute drive from Shute Harbour, where boats leave for various islands (including Hamilton) as well as on snorkel and dive trips to the Great Barrier Reef. In the peak season, a lively mix of visitors swells the ranks of Airlie's population of 3,000 or so, including lots of backpackers, diving enthusiasts and the yachting fraternity – but they haven't entirely robbed Airlie Beach of its charm.

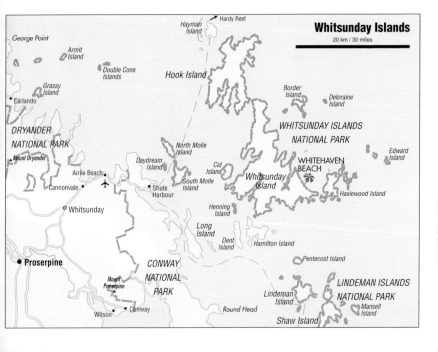

Whitsunday Islands

20 km / 30 miles

Cruise to Reefworld

The one thing visitors should not miss – whether staying at Airlie Beach, Hamilton and any one of the inhabited islands – is the catamaran day trip to **Reefworld** by **FantaSea Cruises** (tel: 07 4946 5111; www.fantasea.com.au). FantaSea also operates the Blue Ferries that service Shute Harbour and the various islands in the Whitsundays. Snorkelling gear is provided on the Reefworld cruise and if you intend to dive, be sure to bring your dive certificate.

You have two choices for the journey to Reefworld – FantaSea Cruise catamaran both ways, or helicopter out and catamaran back. Naturally the second is the more expensive option, but it does give you a dazzling half-hour scenic overview of the Whitsundays.

Reefworld is the name of the huge floating pontoon at **Hardy Reef**, which provides a base for snorkelling, diving and underwater viewing from semi-submersibles or flat-bottom boats. If you've chosen the catamaran, it departs Shute Harbour at 8am (bus pick-ups from Airlie Beach are included) and picks up passengers from Hamilton Island at 8.40am.

Whichever route you take, you'll have marvellous views of the Whitsunday islands. Reefworld's pontoon is designed to offer everyone a rewarding reef experience. You can dive, of course, and there's a guided snorkelling tour with a reef interpreter, but if you'd rather stay dry you can view the diverse coral and reef fish from the safety of the huge underwater viewing chamber or from a semi-submersible. There are safe swimming enclosures for children, and you can lounge on spacious open sundecks with plenty of shaded areas. Facilities include freshwater showers and changing rooms, and a buffet lunch plus morning and afternoon tea is included in the price.

The catamaran leaves Reefworld at 4.05pm and lands you at Hamilton Island at 4.15pm and Shute Harbour at 5.10pm.

Whitehaven Beach

Another must-see whether staying at Airlie Beach or Hamilton Island, is the almost blinding white sands of **Whitehaven Beach** on Whitsunday Island, the largest of the islands in the group. If you're doing this cruise from Airlie Beach, book the **Two-Island Cruise** with Fantasea Cruises. The ferry departs Shute Habour at 9.35am and arrives on Hamilton at 10.05am. It allows passengers about 2½ hours to enjoy the island before picking up guests staying at Hamilton for the trip to Whitehaven Beach. An all-you-can-eat buffet lunch is served on the way as the vessel cruises past a series of islands, the route varying according to the weather. You will be transferred ashore by the catamaran's small landing barge – you won't need shoes – onto one of the world's most perfect beaches, famous for its 6km (4 miles) of glistening white silica sand and sparkling blue water.

Above Left: sailboat, Hamilton Island
Right: picnic on pristine Whitehaven Beach, Whitsunday Island

Whitehaven is a shallow, safe beach that is so long it never seems crowded, despite the number of cruise boats and private vessels that make a landfall here during the peak season. The FantaSea staff will set up a beach volleyball net for the energetic, and sell drinks from a cooler (so take some change). If you've forgotten your swimwear, the northern end of the beach appears to be popular with the more broadminded sunbather. You need to be back with the rest of the party for the 3.45pm departure, first to drop passengers off at Hamilton before making the return journey to Shute Harbour, with an arrival time of 5.10pm.

Bareboat Charters

The Whitsundays is the perfect place to bareboat (meaning sailing a boat yourself) so visitors should consider this if they decide not to base themselves on Airlie Beach or an island. No licence is required but it helps if you have had some experience at the helm of a boat before. You will be given a detailed 2-3 hour briefing on using charts, tide tables and simple navigation instruments. Contact is made on scheduled radio calls twice a day and after-hours assistance is also available. The waters around the Whitsundays are not crowded and generally not difficult to navigate. If still not confident, you can ask for a skipper to be on board with you for the first day (for an extra fee) to show you the ropes. Boats are typically fitted with cabins for 2-8 passengers, with a kitchen, hot showers and toilets. **Queensland Yacht Charters** (07 4946 7400; www.yachtcharters.com.au) and **Whitsunday Rent-A-Yacht** (07 4946 9232; www.rentayacht.com.au) are some of the better known bareboat charters.

excursions

5. HERON ISLAND *(see pull-out map)*

Stay on a coral island on the Tropic of Capricorn and get close to nature. Learn about the ecosystems of the Great Barrier Reef and experience some of the best diving in the world, plus some land-based attractions.

Book a return flight with Sunstate Airlines (book through Qantas tel: 131313; www.qantas.com.au) from Cairns to Gladstone, the mainland jump-off point for Heron Island. Reserve at least three nights at Heron Island (tel: 1800 737 678; www.poresorts.com). Book either the two-hour ferry or 30-minute helicopter trip to Heron. Depending on what time you arrive, you'll either transfer immediately to the helicopter (no flights after dark) or take a taxi into Gladstone (10 minutes) for an overnight stay (try Country Plaza International, 100 Goondoon Street, tel: 07 4972 4499) before taking the ferry from the marina at 11am next morning (check-in 10.30am latest). Bear in mind that Heron Island is on Daylight Saving Time (one hour ahead) all year through. Bring your diving certificate (if you have one), beachwear and smart casual clothing for evenings, camera and binoculars.

Before making a decision about how to travel the 72km (45 miles) from Gladstone to Heron Island, bear in mind that the ferry crossing can be choppy enough for there to be seasickness medication permanently on board. The alternative helicopter ride has a baggage limit of 15kg (33lbs) plus one piece of hand luggage, but excess baggage can be transported on the ferry. Stuff that you don't need can be left at the helicopter operator's office or at the Heron Island office at the marina.

Heron Highlights

However you decide to travel, your stay on **Heron Island** will be a unique experience. It is one of the few resorts where you can walk straight from your room to the Great Barrier Reef and look into waters that are teeming with marine life. This was the first coral reef in Australia to be declared a Marine National Park and is now a World Heritage Site. Queensland University operates a **Research Station** on the island and the resort can arrange a tour for you.

There are several categories of accommodation available at Heron Island, from budget-priced cabins to luxury suites, all with a tropical village atmosphere. The rate is inclusive of all meals and some of the talks and activities. At the time of going to press, price ranges for the five categories of rooms range from AU\$240 to AU\$470 per person (twin sharing) per night; the return fares (per adult) cost AU\$180 for the ferry and AU\$495 for the helicopter.

There is entertainment in the Pandanus Lounge, which has panoramic views of the reef, but above all, this resort is dedicated to learning about and caring for its unique environment. In addition to talks on the island's

Above Left: Hamilton's Beach Club pool at sunset
Left: aerial view of Hamilton Island. **Above:** Heron Island reef

ecology, you will find no telephones or TVs here, no rubbish (it's all transported back to the mainland for disposal) and optimum use of recycled materials. A pay phone is available for emergencies in the reception area.

Seasonal attractions

Though it takes only 30 minutes to walk around the 17-ha (42-acre) island, this beautiful coral cay is a real nature lover's paradise. No matter which month you visit, there is always something interesting to see and experts on hand to explain it all. For instance, between October and May it is Green Turtle time; you can watch these protected species mating, nesting and (from January) see the thousands of tiny turtles hatch and make a dash across the sand to the sea, truly an amazing sight.

In November or December, for a few nights around the full moon, mass coral spawning occurs and the waters are filled with a spectacular display that resembles fireworks, or an upside-down snowstorm – an utterly unforgettable sight. If you're there between June and September, you are quite likely to see humpback whales passing by on their annual migration. All year round, the island is home to a huge number of bird species, and its waters are home to 1,200 of the 1,500 species of fish that inhabit the Great Barrier Reef.

Reef activities

Some of Australia's best dive spots – including the world-famous Bommie – are at Heron. There are 21 different sites, all within about 15 minutes of the jetty. The staff and dive instructors at the resort's Marine Centre are a mine of information, and you can book lessons, charters and tours, and hire boats and equipment for diving. Make sure you allow enough hours to explore the reef with all its brilliant coral formations and fabulous fish. And when you run out of daylight hours, you could try a night dive.

As well as swimming and snorkelling, there are many other activities to enjoy, including a guided underwater tour in Heron's semi-submersible, reef fishing, day and overnight guided camping trips to nearby **Wilson Island**, guided reef and island walks, and even star-gazing from the beach (particularly fascinating for visitors from the northern hemisphere). Heron also operates a terrific Kids Junior Ranger programme, which is tailor-made for 7- to 12-year-olds. A variety of hands-on activities are designed to introduce children to the need for looking after ecologically sensitive environments, while having lots of fun.

Check-out time is 10am, but you have the use of the departure lounge (with shower facilities), so that you can enjoy the island to the full until it's time to leave. The ferry departs at 2pm (Heron Island time) and arrives at Gladstone at 3.45pm (standard time), and the airport shuttle will get you to the airport in time for any flight after 4.20pm. If not, you will have to spend another night in Gladstone.

Above: baby Green Turtles hatch between October and May
Right: learning the ropes from mum

Leisure Activities

OUTDOOR ACTIVITIES

This part of Australia is famous for its outdoor activities, particularly diving and snorkelling, and for adventure sports – if you could copyright the phrase 'adrenaline rush', you'd make a fortune here. A good contact point for such activity is **The Adventure Company Australia** (tel: 07 4051 4777; www.adventures.com.au), which offers nature-based adventures including hiking and diving, or a 4WD Great Northern Safari, taking in Cooktown, Lakefield National Park, Laura Safari Camp and returning via Cape Tribulation.

Learning to Dive

Of all the ways to enjoy the beauty of the Great Barrier Reef, diving among the corals and the fish remains the ultimate, so don't consign this possibility to the 'too difficult basket'. If you're uncertain or confused by the maze of courses and the apparent complexity of the equipment, try a quick introductory diving course and escorted dive, which is an optional extra on one-day reef tours such as Quicksilver's *(see page 48)*. You only need to be a modestly good swimmer, in reasonable general health and free of illnesses such as diabetes, asthma and epilepsy. In just three to four days you can become a qualified diver with the papers to prove it.

Diving in the region is highly organised, and you can trust any of the large number of established operators to deliver quality training, complete safety and a well-earned diver's certificate with loads of fun thrown in as well. The lowest age for a course is 14, and there's no upper age limit, but you need to pass a non-strenuous medical examination. You then do (typically) two days of combined classroom and underwater training in a pool, followed by one or two days of open-water dives under supervision. The course teaches you all about the equipment and its care and use, proper breathing and underwater safety procedures and rules, and leads up to the first level of qualification – the 'open-water diver' certificate.

Before beginning any course, you'll need to provide two passport-sized photographs (for your diver ID) and a medical certificate; the operator can arrange this for you for about AU$50. With your certificate in the kit bag, you can choose from a large range of diving day trips or extended liveaboard cruises.

Below is a selection of recommended dive schools. These provide a range of dive courses as well as organised dive trips. Prices are between AU$300–600 for courses that include open-water diving on day trips; more expensive courses include on-board accommodation and meals.

Cairns

Cairns Dive Centre
Tel: 07 4051 0294
www.cairnsdive.com.au

Deep Sea Divers Den
Tel: 07 4031 2223
www.divers-den.com

Prodive
Tel: 07 4031 5255
www.prodive-cairns.com.au

Tusa Dive
Tel: 07 4031 1248
www.tusadive.com

Port Douglas

Undersea Explorer
Tel: 07 4099 5911
www.undersea.com.au

Left: a novice diver takes the plunge
Right: encountering an underwater world

Mission Beach

Calypso Dive
Tel: 07 4068 8432
www.quickcatdive.com.au

Mission Beach Dive Charters
Tel: 07 4068 7277
www.missiondive.com.au

Snorkelling

There are countless options for snorkelling. Most operators, whether based in Cairns or Port Douglas, will arrange to transfer you to the launch-point of the trip. Apart from snorkelling, most boats also offer dive options, with special introductory dives for novices who are not ready to commit to a certified dive course. A few of the larger boats also offer glass-bottomed boats and semi-submersible craft for those who want to experience the reef without getting wet.

Full-day snorkelling trips which give you up to five hours on the reef, with visits of up to three separate reef sites as well as lunch and hotel pick-up, cost between AU$86–190. The larger (and faster) boats with their own pontoons on the reef normally cost more.

Cairns

Down Under Dive
Tel: 07 4052 8300
www.downunderdive.com.au
With only 80 passengers, the 19-m (62-ft) MV *Supercat* allows for more personal service.

Ocean Spirit Cruises
Tel: 07 4031 2920
www.oceanspirit.com.au
Offers trips on a large comfortable sailing catamaran to Michaelmas and Upolu cays.

Sunlover Cruises
Tel: 07 4050 1333
www.sunlover.com.au
Operates two huge 34-m (111-ft) catamarans which take up to 300 passengers. Trips go out to Arlington Reef and Moore Reef.

Port Douglas

Poseidon Cruises
Tel: 07 4099 4772
www.poseidon-cruises.com.au
The 24-m (78-ft) 70-passenger *Poseidon* visits three outer barrier reef sites. This is one of the better mid-priced operations.

Quicksilver Connections
Tel: 07 4087 2100
www.quicksilver-cruises.com
Apart from its *Wavepiercer* described on pages 48–49, Quicksilver also operates four other vessels to different parts of the reef.

Wavelength
Tel: 07 4099 5031
www.wavelength.com.au
Excellent for first-timers and experienced snorkellers. Efficient and helpful staff help put the nervous at ease. Takes only 30 passengers maximum.

Hot-air Ballooning

Drifting silently over the Atherton Table-lands in the placid early morning air is an awesome experience. It's well worth the early start, which is typically a 4.30am pick-up at your Cairns hotel for a one-hour drive to Mareeba. The crew will have the balloon just about ready when you arrive. You're guaranteed a fine view, because ballooning is only possible in near-calm conditions; and you're usually airborne close to sunrise.

Ballooning is inextricably associated with champagne breakfasts, which are included in the package by all operators. It is also possible to combine the ballooning experience with other adventure activities, such as white-water rafting and skydiving, or with visits to well-known tourist attractions.

Three operators offer flights of 30 minutes' or an hour's duration in the Mareeba area, inclusive of pick-up and return to Cairns, and a champagne breakfast.

'disembarkation' options from higher altitudes up to about 4,300m (14,000ft) with incremental pricing, and videos recording your few moments of free-fall. Prices are typically around AU$250 for a jump from 2,500m (8,000ft), plus AU$48 for every 600m (2,000ft) you increase the jump height.

Cairns

Champagne Balloon Flights
Tel: 07 4058 1688
www.champagneballoons.com.au

Hot Air
Tel: 07 4039 2900
www.hotair.com.au

Raging Thunder
Tel: 07 4030 7900
www.ragingthunder.com.au

Tandem Parachuting

It may not seem like it to some, but there's actually a lot of fun in strapping yourself to an experienced skydiver, donning a pair of goggles, leaping out of an aeroplane, and plummeting from 2,500m (8,000ft) or more while admiring the view and wondering when, or if, the parachute's going to open.

This memorable experience attracts thousands of visitors every year, and a typical package includes pick-up and return to your hotel, a safety briefing, a scenic ascent, and the Big Moment. The first part is a free-fall descent for a minute or so, then a more leisurely glide after your sports parachute opens. At the planned destination, a recovery team awaits. Most operators offer

Cairns

Paul's Parachuting
Tel: 07 4051 8855
www.paulsparchuting.com.au
Departs from Cairns airport and recovers you from a drop zone at Edmonton, 12km (7 miles) south.

Skydive Cairns
Tel: 07 4031 5466
www.skydivecairns.com.au
Also flies from Cairns airport and recovers you from a (different) drop zone at Edmonton.

Mission Beach

Skydive Mission Beach
Tel: 07 4052 1822
www.jumptthebeach.com
Takes off from Tully airport and lands you on Mission Beach or Dunk Island.

White-water Rafting

Experienced guides raft you down rapidly flowing rivers, graded according to the degree of difficulty, in (usually) full-day expeditions that combine stunning scenery, excitement and an outdoor lunch. The fact that you have to sign a liability release form before you set off indicates a possibility of minor injury, but this usually only happens

Left: snorkellers get a feel of the waters from the *Wavepiercer*'s pontoon
Above: hot-air ballooning is an option for those afraid of the water

to people who don't follow instructions. Rafts carry up to seven passengers in addition to the guide, and prices are typically around AU$85 for a half-day and AU$130 for a full-day, including lunch.

Cairns

Foaming Fury
Tel: 07 3031 3460
www.foamingfury.com.au
Half-day trips on the Barron River, and full-day 'walk-in-raft-out' trips on the Russel River (near Innisfail) in which you carry a light pack on a 40-minute rainforest walk.

Raging Thunder
Tel: 07 4030 7900
www.ragingthunder.com.au
Half-day trips on the Barron River (Cairns), day-trips on the Tully River two hours south of Cairns and a full day sea kayaking adventure on the Great Barrier Reef. This company also picks up at Port Douglas and Mission Beach.

Bungy Jumping
Australians will tell you that only a New Zealander could dream this up. Hurtling earthwards head-first won't make your eyes pop out, but the rapid reduction from 95kph (59mph) to zero terminal velocity is certainly an experience.

A J Hackett Bungy (tel: 07 4057 7188; www.ajhackett. com.au) invites you to step into space from its 50-m (164-ft) tower, high in the rainforest, with your heart in your mouth and nothing in your pockets. The tension of the big elastic band can be adjusted so your head dips in the pool below at the end of the fall!

Scenic Flights
Don't miss an aerial overview of the Great Barrier Reef. Scenic flight operators offer circuits of the coastline to Cape Tribulation, returning via the outer reef. Flights depart from their premises at the general aviation area on the western side of the Cairns airport.

Cairns

Cairns Tiger Moth Scenic Flights
Tel: 07 4035 9400
Pilot Justin Meadows flies a 1931 DH82 open cockpit bi-plane over Cairns and the beaches.

Sunlover Helicopters
Tel: 07 4035 9669
www.gbrhelicopters.com.au
Provides a range of experiences, some of them packaged with four-wheel-drive and reef experiences and visits to spectacular but otherwise inaccessible areas.

Sailing
The Cairns Yacht Club has a club race every Wednesday and invites visitors along as crew for a modest AU$10, which includes a sausage sizzle and a cold drink. Be there at 12 noon (tel: 07 4031 2750).

Fishing
Anything between dangling a line from a jetty and a full-on endurance battle with the region's legendary black marlin is possible on Queensland's east coast. You can hire tackle and buy bait close to most boat ramps, hire a dinghy in Cairns, or drive to the beaches and coastal headlands to fish.

For more serious fishing, go with a fully-equipped and knowledgeable guide. While encouraging a 'catch and release' practice, the guide won't object if you take a fish home for dinner; and will even clean it for you.

Cairns

Cairns Reef Charter Services
Tel: 07 4031 4742
www.ausfish.com/crcs/

Catcha Crab
Tel: 07 4051 7992
www.catcha-crab.com
Offers the chance to catch and enjoy eating your own delicious Queensland mud crab.

Left: seaplane rides for aerial overviews

always popular. Genuine returning models (as opposed to the strictly ornamental variety) come with instructions on how to throw them properly.

Didgeridoos, the Aboriginal musical instrument produced from tree branches hollowed out by termites, are also popular. It's said that the average Qantas flight leaving Australia carries enough didgeridoos to start a *corroboree* (Aboriginal ceremonial dance). Didgeridoos were designed before overhead lockers were invented, so do check them in with your baggage. The **Tjapukai Aboriginal Gallery**, adjacent to the cultural park, (*see page 33*) is a showplace of authentic Aboriginal art and artefacts.

Books
There's a good cross-section of books on local history (some self-published), natural history, rainforest flora and fauna at the **Cairns Museum Gift Shop** in City Place.

Clothing
Among the most popular Australian clothing lines is **Akubra**, whose famous broad-brimmed felt hats are hugely popular with overseas visitors. You can pick one up at **Australian Outback** shop at the Pier Marketplace, along with leather bush hats, oil-skin coats made famous in the movie *The Man from Snowy River*, and of course, crocodile products. **R M Williams** is known for the rugged-looking bushwear that he's designed for rural people for many years, which has become internationally known, particularly the riding boots and Driza Bone raincoats.

Artist **Ken Done** and his designer wife produce light and bright casual clothes sold

SHOPPING

In parts of North Queensland, you may get the feeling that there's a shop to fit every every customer profile. This keen competition is not a bad thing for bargain-hunters because it holds prices down. Big shopping centres – mostly found in Cairns – which incorporate supermarkets and speciality shops, are home to dozens of the most notable names in Australian retail. Parking is free and relatively easy, and prices tend to be more attuned to domestic shoppers than to grabbing tourist dollars.

Among the most rewarding shopping is looking for exclusively Australian products (but beware of Southeast Asian fakes), and these include timber art, fashion, jewellery, music, art works, leather products and pure wool garments. Cairns is also the T-shirt capital of Australia, emblazoned with humorous images focusing on activities such as drinking beer, engaging with the opposite gender, or being devoured by crocodiles.

Cairns
Aboriginal Artefacts
Some Aboriginal artefacts are 'fair dinkum' (genuine) and some are mass-produced. For the former, try boomerangs, which are

Above: eye-catching bags
Right: stuffed koalas make nice souvenirs

at their 4 Spence Street shop in Cairns. **Brothers Neilsen** is a brand specialising in Australian-designed casual street, beach and surf wear as well as surfboards. **Emaroo** produces a range of designer fashion knit-wear made from pure Australian wool or cotton; lambswool lined **UGG Boots** are popular with visitors returning to colder climates; and **Brian Rochford** is a popular Australian label for skimpy swimwear.

Crafts and Jewellery

Queensland's richly-coloured boulder opals are in ever-growing demand; as are the large and lustrous Australian South Sea pearls. Creative jewellers use them together with Australian Argyle coloured diamonds, ranging in hue from 'champagne' and 'cognac' to the rarer pinks. Such treasures are best bought from a reputable jeweller.

Now that crocodiles and emus are farmed, their by-products are widely available. Hand-bags, belts, wallets and backscratchers are among the most popular products, as are sheepskin rugs made from the hides of Australia's famous merino sheep. Another speciality are emu eggs – the shells have seven different layers of colour, ranging from dark green to white, and skilful carving (Aborigines are expert at this) produces beautiful intricate patterns. Here is just a selection from the great many outlets in the area:

Australian Geographic
Pier Marketplace, Cairns
Tel: 07 4041 6211
'Australiana' gifts, books, music, children's educational toys, outdoor equipment. An Australian gift for anybody back home.

Australian Gold Nugget Jewellery
Pier Marketplace, Cairns

Gold nuggets as they come from the earth, cleaned of dirt and rock, and made into a wide range of jewellery. Each piece is unique and comes with a certificate.

Night Pearls
Night Markets, The Esplanade, Cairns
You choose an oyster from the tank and it's opened to reveal your pearl – with the proviso that if you don't like that particular pearl, you can exchange it for one from their 'pearl bank'. It can then be mounted on any of the settings available.

Peter Lik's Wilderness Gallery
4 Shields Street, Cairns
Tel: 07 4031 8177
www.peterlik.com
A remarkable collection of limited edition photographic prints depicting Australia in all its visual facets. This well-known photographer also produces postcards, widely available throughout the region (including here). Open daily 9am–10pm.

The Chalet Rainforest Gallery
Gillies Highway, Yungaburra
Tel: 07 4095 2144
The only outlet for 'Rainforest Folk', created by doll-maker Chris Boston. Open daily 8.30am–5pm. See also page 39.

Duty-free Shopping

Apart from the usual airport outlets, there's the **DFS Galleria** at the corner of Abbott and Spence streets (www.dfsgalleria.com; daily 8.30am–10pm), which is centrally located and provides a free shuttle bus 2–10pm. Goods here are up to 10 percent cheaper than at the airport, but as your package is sealed at the shop, you have to wait until you are out of the country before you can break into it. A docket is attached, which will be inspected by customs officials when you leave.

Food and Drink

Australian-produced foodstuffs are becoming increasingly popular. These include macadamia nuts, native to Australia and formerly called the Queensland nut. Many outlets sell macadamia nuts in a variety of guises, including chocolates and biscuits. There is also tea and coffee from plantations

Left: quirky 'Rainforest Folk'

Located at the western end of Shields Street. Open weekdays 9am–5.30pm (until 9pm Thur); weekends 10am–4pm.

Pier Marketplace
Pierpoint Road
Tel: 07 4051 7244
You can't miss it, because it dominates the seaward view from the Esplanade. Open daily 9am–9pm.

Smithfield Centre
Tel: 07 4038 1006
At the corner of the Cook and Kennedy highways, by the Smithfield roundabout. Trading hours vary. Phone for information.

Stockland Earlville
537 Mulgrave Road
Tel: 07 4054 3066
Trading hours vary. Phone for information.

Markets
Cairns Night Markets and Food Court
56 Abbott Street through to the Esplanade
Open daily 4.30–11pm.

The Mud Markets
Pier Marketplace, Pierpoint Road, Cairns
Local handicrafts in the shopping centre's open spaces. Every weekend 8am–4pm.

Rusty's Bazaar Market
57–89 Grafton Street, Cairns
Friday 6am–6pm, Saturday and Sunday 6am–2pm.

Kuranda 'Original' Market
5 Therwine Street, Kuranda
Open Wednesday, Thursday, Friday and Sunday 9am–4pm.

Kuranda 'Heritage' Market
Rob Veivers Drive, Kuranda
Open every day during daylight hours.

Yungaburra Market
Yungaburra
This is the best market of all. Have a cup of tea and a sandwich with the ladies of the Country Women's Association in their hall opposite the park. Held every fourth Saturday of the month, in the morning.

in Tropical North Queensland, koala-shaped pasta and, for adventurous carnivores, crocodile, shark or emu jerky. Australian wine and beer is now available all over the world, but browse around bottle shops for local varieties *(see Eating Out, page 80)*.

Natural Remedies
Emu oil, naturally high in Vitamin E and known for its penetrating ability, is popular with massage therapists. It has been shown to reduce pain, swelling and stiffness in joints, and helps ease sports-related injuries when used sparingly.

Goanna salve and goanna oil, despite the names, are manufactured only from native Australian plants, and were first produced in Queensland in 1910 to relieve aches and pains. Tea-tree oil, avocado cream and lanolin (from wool) products, are all designed to ease, soften and soothe, and are used in a variety of lotions and creams.

Shopping Centres
The main centres for shopping in Cairns are as follows:

Cairns Central
McLeod Street
Tel: 07 4041 4111

Above: a Kuranda market vendor with an array of sharks' teeth

EATING OUT

Australia's gastronomic credentials are born of two factors – the cultural diversity which brought some of the world's best cooking talent here, and the richness and variety of the culinary resources these cooks found at their fingertips. It includes (according to Australians) the tenderest, juiciest and tastiest steak, the most delicious fish (barramundi, closely followed by coral trout) and an endless variety of fresh and flavourful garden and farm produce.

Don't be surprised if some of the best restaurants bear intercontinental names. Without looking far, you'll find American, Australian, British, Chinese, Egyptian, French, German, Greek, Indian, Indonesian, Irish, Italian, Japanese, Latin American, Mexican, Middle Eastern, Spanish, Swiss and Thai restaurants (whew!), and various hybrids of those.

The variety of Queensland seafood is excellent, usually fresh and very popular, but there's also a good selection for meatlovers (including indigenous varieties such as emu, crocodile and kangaroo), as well as vegetarian options, with superb fresh produce from the Atherton Tablelands.

If you want to eat alfresco, dozens of outlets around Cairns offer good quality takeaway food; a popular area is the 2.5-km (1¼-mile) Esplanade (called the 'Nard' by locals). 'Fish 'n' Chips 'n' Fourex' (XXXX beer) is a popular combination, and if you have the ingredients, there are gas-fired barbecues scattered along the shoreline for an impromptu 'barbie'.

Australian Wines

The reputation of Australian wines has now fully matured, and the range is growing every year as more new vineyards spring up. The stiff competition also helps keep good wines affordable on the home front. At a recent Cairns wine show, well-known Australian wine critic Andrew Corrigan awarded the accolade for 'the best wine for tropical enjoyment' to the Pokolbin Estate 2000 Hunter Riesling, from the Hunter Valley in New South Wales. Such light, fruity and lemony wines have a zingy freshness that complements North Queensland seafood.

As a guideline, the best oak-driven reds or whites come from the oldest-established Barossa Valley in South Australia, while the Hunter Valley is highly popular for its fruity Chardonnay and Pinot Noir.

There are good reds everywhere, but this biased judge believes the finest come from Northern Victoria – Plunkett Wines' award-winning Strathbogie Ranges Shiraz, Chateau Tahbilk's well-oaked Cabernet Sauvignon, Morris's richly flavoured and thickly textured reds from Rutherglen, and Baileys Block Shiraz ('a rump steak in every glass' according to one critic) from Glenrowan.

Many a fine but unlicensed restaurant falls into the BYO (bring your own) category – you buy your wine from a convenient bottle shop and it's decanted for you at the restaurant with no corkage charge. At the bottle shops, don't be deterred from trying the economical, often highly palatable cask wines, (known in Aussiespeak as 'château cardboard'). A good, rich red in this category is Morris's Pressings Dry Red, with a full flavoured palate, originating from the Rutherglen region in northern Victoria.

Beers

Australian beers are famous internationally, and are patriotically consumed in vast quantities by their domestic devotees. The most popular are: Victoria Bitter, a slightly darker-than-usual full strength beer with characteristic maltiness and a full flavour; Crown Lager, a creamy, fruity lager; and XXXX Bitter ('Fourex'). Queensland's detractors claim that this name was allocated because few Queenslanders could spell 'beer'. Several varieties of 'light' beer are also available.

Above: yummy oysters are best eaten raw

Restaurants

Quality food in Australia is eminently affordable. In the restaurant recommendations below, price ranges for a three-course dinner for two, without wine, are as follows:

$ = below AU\$50
$$ = between AU\$50–80
$$$ = above AU\$80

Cairns

There are plenty of alternatives to hotel restaurants (which generally offer dining of a quality closely linked to their room rates), away from most of the backpacker hustle and bustle. If you're looking for something more conducive to conversation, with, perhaps, a tropical backdrop, you'll find plenty of choice along the waterfront. Some offer a 30 percent 'early bird' discount (not including drinks) to customers seated before 6.30pm.

Cairns Yacht Club
4 The Esplanade
Tel: 07 4031 2750
Unsophisticated and inexpensive Aussie cuisine in informal surroundings, with an emphasis on steak and seafood. As long as your clothing includes footwear, a member will sign you in. The restaurant is best approached on foot because parking is always a problem. Happy Hour every day 5.30–6.30pm. Lunch 12–2pm, dinner 5.30–8pm. $

Café China
Rydges Plaza Complex, corner of Spence Street and Grafton Street
Tel: 07 4041 2828
Delicious Peking and Cantonese cuisine, dim sum (yum cha), seafood and noodles cooked in a healthy low-fat style. Owner Harry Sou makes sure that diners are well looked after. Open daily for lunch and dinner $$

Donnini's Ciao Italia
Pier Marketplace
Tel: 07 4051 1133
Consistently good and value-for-money Italian food, with special highlights listed on the daily specials board. Open kitchen allows diners to see everything that is going on. Friendly, helpful service. Open daily for lunch and dinner. $$

Right: take your pick of fresh seafood

Faculty of Tourism & Hospitality
Institute of Technical & Further Education Campus, Gatton Street, Manunda
Tel: 07 4042 2664
If you're impressed by the region's culinary diversity, track it to one of its sources. Only available during school terms, this unusual venue provides a chance for well-supervised hospitality students to practise on real live customers. If they appear a little nervous, it's probably exam time. Quite an experience! Lunch only, bookings necessary. $

Mondo's Café Bar & Grill
Hilton Hotel
Tel: 07 4052 6780
Close to the city and with prime waterfront views, this place is also great for coffee amidst palms and poinciana, with mangroves across the water. Its broad ranging menu of international dishes emphasises local produce. The dinner barbecue is especially recommended. Open lunch noon–2.30pm; dinner 6–10pm. $$

P J O'Brien's
83 Lake Street
Tel: 07 4031 5333
It's not only the Irish who will enjoy a night here. Apart from grilled barramundi, and a wide choice of steaks and lamb dishes, this cheerful venue has an Irish fare menu (including the famous stew), naturally to be washed down with a pint of Guinness. 'Irish hours' 11.30am–3pm, dinner 5.30–8pm. $$

Raw Prawn
103 The Esplanade
Tel: 07 4031 5400
Peter Horn's menu includes extensive fish and crustacea selections prepared in Australian styles. Begin with a bloody Mary oyster shooter, followed by a starter of smoked kangaroo, cured crocodile and emu pâté with a Caesar salad, and for a main course go for wild barramundi, gulf prawns and Moreton Bay bug meat fried in tempura batter and served with salad and fruit. Daily 5–10pm. $$$

Red Ochre Grill
43 Shields Street
Tel: 07 4051 0100
'Creative Native Australian cuisine' is offered on an inventive menu that uses up to 40 different native ingredients to enhance dishes such as emu, kangaroo, crocodile, tropical fruit and seafoods. Try the kangaroo sirloin with chilli glaze, and for dessert, wattleseed pavlova with mango sauce. *$$$*

Strait On The Beach
100 Oleander Street, Holloway's Beach
Tel: 07 40559616
Oddly, this beachfront eatery, a 10-minute drive from Cairns CBD, does breakfast and lunch but not dinner, except takeaways. Good coffee and croissants for breakfast. Open daily 7.30am–7pm. *$*

Villa Romano Trattoria
Corner of Aplin Street and the Esplanade
Tel: 07 4051 9000
In this restaurant everything on the menu has an Italian name, including the Carpentaria Gulf prawns, the Darling Downs beef fillets, and the barramundi, cooked the way only the Italians can do it. There is also a selection of Japanese dishes, and an outside seating area. Daily 6.30am–11pm. *$$$*

Yanni's Greek Taverna
Corner of Aplin Street and Grafton Street
Tel: 07 4041 1500
Traditional Greek and Mediterranean cuisine in authentic surroundings. Belly dancing and plate smashing on Friday and Saturday nights. Indoor or coutryard dining available.

Palm Cove

Casma Café and Bar
73 Williams Esplanade (corner with Harpa Street)
Tel: 07 4059 0013
Reserve early for a table by the breezy balcony on the first floor. Delicious and innovative contemporary Australian cuisine with Asian accents. Everything on the menu is good but ask the waitstaff to recommend. *$$*

Far Horizons
Angsana Resort & Spa, 1 Vievers Road
Tel: 07 4055 3090
Absolute beach frontage with waving coconut palms in attendance lend tropical charm to an innovative menu rich in local produce – fresh seafood caught in local waters and delicacies from the market gardens of the Atherton Tablelands. *$$$*

Reef House Restaurant
Sebel Reef House, 99 Williams Esplanade
Tel: 07 4055 3633
Subtle Asian and Mediterranean flavours enhance seafood, beef and chicken dishes – and you have a choice of either beach or pool views. Start with scorched sea scallop, and have the crispy ocean trout fillet for the main course. Attentive service and a fine wine list make for a romantic night out. *$$$*

Port Douglas

Mango Jam
24 Macrossan Street
Tel: 07 4099 4611
This always busy eatery offers value-for-money meals. Wonderful selection of gourmet wood-fired pizzas, many with Asian-inspired toppings like tandoori chicken and spicy Thai prawns, and mains like chargrilled leg of lamb and Porterhouse steak with caramelised onion jam. Ask for the specials of the day. *$$*

Michelangelo's
26 Macrossan Street
Tel: 07 4099 4663
Wood fired pizza and pasta lounge bar, popular with the locals. The chilli mussels with white wine and pomodoro tomatoes is highly recommended. Open 11am till late. *$$*

On The Inlet
3 Inlet Street
Tel: 07 4099 5255
'Sunset Special' between 4 and 6pm offers oysters or a bucket of prawns while you're watching the sun set over the jungle-clad ranges behind Mossman Gorge. The pier-front restaurant then resumes its role as one of the 'Port's' premier restaurants, with a strong emphasis on fresh seafood caught locally. Open daily from noon–late. *$$$*

Salsa Bar and Grill
26 Wharf Street
Tel: 07 4099 4922
A blend of Pacific rim, Mediterranean and Asian flavours is on offer here. For starters, tiger prawn and goat cheese empanada, followed by fried barramundi with coconut rice, and bok choy with kaffir lime cream sauce. Their famous margaritas go well with the chocolate cointreau soufflé. Open daily from noon–midnight. *$$–$$$*

Mission Beach

Blarney's by the Beach
10 Wongaling Beach Road
Tel: 07 4068 8472
This is an upmarket à la carte restaurant. Try the crispy roast duck with orange and cointreau sauce or a whole roast rack of lamb. Open Tues–Sat and Sun lunch. *$$$*

The Horizon at Mission Beach
Explorer Drive, South Mission Beach
Tel: 07 4068 8154
With fine views of Dunk Island, this superlative venue specialises in (but is not limited to) seafood dishes. If there at the right time, try the full moon seafood feast. *$$$*

Raymond's on the Beach
1, Banfield Parade, Wongaling Beach
Tel: 07 4068 8177
Open for dinner every night, this open air venue offers a range of 'reef and beef' specials. Also a decent list of vegetarian options. Like most eateries in this area, it has fine views of Mission Beach. Happy hour daily 4.30–6.30pm. *$*

Airlie Beach

Armada Lounge Bar & Restaurant
350 Shute Harbour Road
Tel: 07 4948 1600
International-style dishes and modern lounge music, a fine wine list, extravagant cocktails and imported beers. A taste of the city in the tropics. *$$$*

Panache Restaurant and Bar
Shute Harbour Road, Airlie Beach
Tel: 07 4946 6337
This beachside restaurant uses predominantly Australian produce but cooks it with Mediterranean flavours. Try the pork spare ribs, hickory-smoked, sizzled on the char-grill and served with a delicious barbecue sauce. Wines are modestly priced and well-chosen. *$$$*

Left: romantic beachside dining at Reef House Restaurant, Palm Cove
Above: al fresco lunching at Pier Marketplace, Cairns

NIGHTLIFE

Don't look for wall-to-wall sophistication in Northern Queensland. Cairns, Airlie Beach and Mission Beach nightlife focuses on the backpacker party circuit, which revolves around the 'ours-is-louder-than-yours' concept, whether it's indoor nightclubs or open sided pubs. That said, the arts have become respected and valued aspects of the Queensland psyche. Performing arts events range from imported extravaganzas by world-famous entertainers, to happy little (and not so little) local events, at several venues in Cairns, Port Douglas, Kuranda and the Tablelands. The region is also generously endowed with galleries (there is considerable emphasis on indigenous art) and open-air concert venues.

Artistic events are, however, rarely repeat affairs and tend to pop up randomly. To keep apace with what's happening, Arts Nexus, a non-profit-making community arts support association, provides an invaluable service. Their six-weekly quality review (also called *Arts Nexus*) publishes detailed listings of coming events, and can be obtained from their office at Shop 6, The Hilton, Wharf Street, Cairns (www.artsnexus. com.au), opposite the Reef Hotel Casino.

Other listings can be found in Friday's *Cairns Post*, which publishes a pull-out guide called *Time Out*, and the *Time Out Gig Guide* which lists the coming week's action and attractions. *Barfly*, an 'alternative' weekly handout found in pubs and clubs, also lists current activities and entertainment.

Above: a Cairns bar scene
Right: beer by the bottle

Cairns

Cairns City Place
Tel: 07 4044 3715
Stop by the City Place any time you hear music; on Wednesday (7–8pm) and Friday night (7–9pm) you might detect the sounds of the Snake Gully Band or similar local talent.

Fitzroy Island Party Boat
Tel: 07 4030 7907
www.ragingthunder.com.au
A fast catamaran leaves the Reef Fleet Terminal, Cairns at 7pm every Saturday night with bar service. Raging (Aussie for 'partying') occurs at Fitzroy Island's Raging Thunder Beach Bar where booze and buffet are additional. There's a dance floor with a video disco, and the survivors embark for Cairns after midnight. There's also a guided night dive only for the strictly sober, so the numbers are sometimes insufficient.

Gilligans Backpackers, Hotel & Resort
57–98 Grafton Street
Tel: 07 4041 6566
www.gilligansbackpackers.com.au
A new and modern backpacker venue offering nightly entertainment, international acts, live in-house band, games and quiz nights, some with worthwhile prizes.

Johnno's Blues Bar
Corner of Abbott Street and Aplin Street
Tel: 07 4051 8770
One of Cairns' most popular nightspots (for the young). Local and international artists keep the heat on from 6pm until closing time, which is very late.

Ocean Spirit Dinner Cruises
Tel: 07 4031 2920
www.oceanspirit.com.au
Offers evening cruises on a catamaran every night. Cruise Trinity Bay's calm waters while you enjoy a three-course seafood buffet with a glass of champagne. Departs at 7pm and returns at 9.30pm.

Sports Bar Night Club and Café
33 Spence Street
Tel: 07 4041 2533
Specialises in live bands (Thur–Sat), DJ's seven nights a week, and menu meals during the entertainment. An 18–35 age group is predominant.

Sofitel Reef Hotel Casino
35–41 Wharf Street
Tel: 07 4030 8888
www.reefcasino.com.au
The casino has over 500 gaming machines and over 40 tables, four restaurants, a contemporary bar with live entertainment and a nightclub. When you tire of gambling, head for the roof-top Cairns Rainforest Dome, a wildlife park with pythons, frogs, birds, and a 4-m (13-ft) long saltwater crocodile.

Ultimate Party
Tel: 07 4041 0332
Any Saturday night you can indulge in an unashamed pub crawl. Your ticket pays for a bus cruise and cover charges for two bars and three nightclubs for eight hours of non-stop partying, including a 'free shot' on each entry and a pizza to finish the evening.

Port Douglas
Court House Hotel
Macrossan Street
Tel: 07 4099 5181
Live entertainment at weekends, a sunset cocktail lounge, and great pub food. 11am–10pm.

Henry's Place
Marina Mirage
Tel: 07 4099 5200
Complete with bottle shop and bar, Henry's entertainment includes a live band on Monday night and a jam night on Friday. Visitors welcome, BYO instruments.

Iron Bar & Restaurant
5 Macrossan Street
Tel: 07 4099 4776
Named after its structure of galvanised but rusty corrugated iron, the architectural emblem of Australian shearing sheds and outhouses, the Iron Bar's menu includes indigenous dishes such as crocodile and kangaroo. Entertainment is lively.

Nicky G's
Marina Mirage
Tel: 07 4099 5200
A range of theme nights for backpackers, as well as retro nights and live bands every Sunday. The nightclub is popular with the 18–35 age group. Nightly 10pm–5am.

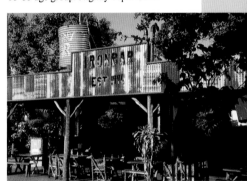

Mossman
Karnak Playhouse and Rainforest Sanctuary
Whyanbeel Road
Tel: 07 4098 8144
Unless you're starting from Port Douglas it's a little out of town, but worth the trip. The playhouse is owned by former film actress Diane Cilento and her late playwright husband, Anthony Shaffer. A range of plays in a magnificent rainforest amphitheatre are presented. Season runs during the dry period from June to December, with performances on every Wednesday and Saturday night.

Airlie Beach
In Queensland's backpacker capital, choose from several nightclubs; there's not much between them, so take your pick from **The Juice Bar**, **303** and **Mama Africa**, all located along Shute Harbour Road.

Right: the rough-and-ready Iron Bar & Restaurant in Port Douglas

CALENDAR OF EVENTS

January/February
On 26 January, a country-wide public holiday marks **Australia Day**. Around the end of the month is the start of the barramundi fishing season (tel: 07 4035 0700).

March/April
Over Easter weekend, there's the annual **Townsville to Dunk Island Race**, a classic blue water yacht race. **Anzac Day** is on the 25 April, when Australian military history is commemorated with dawn services and street parades. The Returned Servicemen's League in Cairns can provide further information (tel: 07 4051 5804). On the same day, the **Diggers' Cup** race meeting takes place at Mareeba (tel: 07 4092 5093).

May
Queensland **Labour Day** is a state holiday on the first Monday, followed shortly by **Cairns Tropical Garden Show**, held at the Cairns Showgrounds (tel: 07 4051 6699). Towards the end of May, you can join in the festivities at the **Port Douglas Village Carnivale** (tel: 07 4099 5066).

June
Queensland Day is on 6 June, commemorating independence from the colony of New South Wales. The week of celebrations includes citizenship ceremonies. The **Queen's Birthday** is celebrated in mid-June, and on the Saturday and Sunday of the long weekend, **Cooktown Discovery Festival** commemorates the landing of Captain Cook on 17 June 1770 with a re-enactment of the event (tel: 07 4069 6004).

Usually after the re-enactment weekend, on a Friday and Saturday, the **Cooktown Annual Race Meeting** is held – which is part of the Peninsular Racing Circuit (tel: 07 4069 5309).

Towards the end of the month, up in Laura on the Cape York Peninsula, is the biennial **Laura Aboriginal and Torres Strait Islander Cultural Festival** (tel: 07 4060 3214). Lots of ethnic and tribal costumes and handicraft displays make this festival especially colourful.

Also in the last week of June is the exciting **Hamilton Outrigger Cup** event (tel: 07 4946 8505). Over 1,000 competitors contest the events and the total prize pool for the 42-km (26-mile) marathon is AU$100,000.

July
There are a whole glut of agricultural shows to be enjoyed this month, starting with the **Malanda Annual Show**, held over two days in the early part of the month at the Malanda Showgrounds (tel: 07 4096 5349).

The **Atherton Annual Show**, another two-day event, follows (tel: 07 4091 4260), with the **Innisfail Annual Show** (tel: 07 4061 3051) and the three-day **Cairns Annual Show** (tel: 07 4051 6699) coming along in mid- to late-July.

Call 07 4035 9438 for details of the **North Queensland Aero Club's Open Day**: a North Queensland Warbirds display, Royal Flying Doctor Service and Queensland Rescue Service are featured, along with scenic and trial instructional flights.

In mid-July, enjoy a weekend of cattle station skills at the **Mareeba Rodeo** at Kerribee Park, Mareeba (tel: 07 4092 1583), or, if golf is more your scene, watch some top golfers compete in the **Pro-Am Golf** tournament at Paradise Palms (tel: 07 4059 1166).

August

On the third Saturday is the **Great Pyramid Race** at Gordonvale (tel: 07 4056 6106). Around the middle of the month there's the **Hamilton Island Yacht Race** week (tel: 07 4946 9999). Exciting **Surf Carnivals** continue through August and September at local and regional beaches (tel: 07 4055 3695).

September

September is springtime, and the Cairns Botanic Gardens holds its **Spring Festival** on the first Sunday in the month (tel: 07 4044 3398). This is also traditionally Father's Day in Australia. In the early part of September Kuranda has its **Kurandafest**, a fun community event (tel: 07 4092 3400).

The first three weeks of the month is when **Festival Cairns** takes place, encompassing the Cairns Amateurs Race Meeting (tel: 07 4041 4911), and street parades (tel: Cairns City Council, 07 4044 3020).

October

The first Saturday in October sees the start of the two-week **Torimba Festival of the Forest** (at Ravenshoe in the Atherton Tablelands), a competitive woodcraft exhibition (tel: Brian Robinson 07 4097 6153).

In the middle of the month there is the **Aquatic Festival**, held in Rotary Park, Wongaling Beach, in the Mission Beach area (tel: 07 4068 2288), and on unspecified dates during this month is the **Lizard Island Black Marlin Fishing Classic** (tel: 07 4031 4742).

November/December

In November, enjoy **Opera in the Outback** under the stars in an amphitheatre at the **Undarra Lava Lodge** (tel: 07 4097 1411), about four hours drive southwest of Cairns on the Gulf Development Road.

Dunk Island's version of the Melbourne Cup, in the form of **horse racing on the beach,** causes great excitement on the first Tuesday in November (tel: 1800 737 678).

The **Whitsunday FantaSea Reef Festival** (tel: 07 4945 3711) blasts off on the first Friday in November with a 'cracker night' (Aussie for fireworks display). Week-long festivities end with a **FantaSea Food Sunday** on the foreshore.

This is also the time of the year for the spectacular **coral spawning** season. You have to be underwater to appreciate this remarkable phenomenon, so contact boat operators in the area for information on night diving and snorkelling.

Left: Mareeba Rodeo takes place in mid-July
Above: concert audience. **Right:** a Pacific Islander adds local colour

Practical Information

GETTING THERE

By Air

Cairns has regular air links to Auckland, Hong Kong, Kuala Lumpur, Port Moresby, Singapore, Taipei, Fukuoka, Nagoya, Osaka and Tokyo, and frequent flights to Brisbane, Sydney and Melbourne, as well as to tourist destinations like Whitsunday Islands, Darwin, Alice Springs and Ayers Rock.

Published fares are high, but off-peak deals are often better than the 30 percent discount for holders of international air tickets. Check with **Qantas** (tel: domestic 131313, international tel: 131211; www.qantas.com). Cairns-based **Australian Airlines** (tel: 1300 799789; www.australianairlines.com.au) flies to the Gold Coast, other state capitals and several Asian destinations. Other competitively priced airlines are **Jetstar** (tel: 131538; www.jetstar.com) and **Virgin Blue** (tel: 136789; www.virginblue.com.au).

The international and domestic terminals are connected by a 400-m (¼-mile) covered walkway. The airport is 8km (5 miles) from central Cairns. Many hotels and resorts provide courtesy coach transfers. A taxi to the central business district costs about AU$13 for a standard cab and AU$20 for a nine-passenger minibus. **Australia Coach** (tel: 07 4048 8355) to Cairns' hotels charge AU$8. **Airport Connection** (tel: 07 4099 5950) services Port Douglas and Mission Beach.

By Rail

The Sunlander service (four times weekly) along the coast from Brisbane to Cairns takes about 31½ hours. The faster Tilt Train (thrice weekly) takes just over 24 hours. The ride is not particularly scenic and offers only two brief glimpses of the coastline (tel: 132232; www.traveltrain.com.au).

By Road

It about 20 hours to drive from Brisbane to Cairns, not including stops. Coach travel takes about 29 hours; contact **McCafferty's Greyhound** (tel: 132030 or 131499).

TRAVEL ESSENTIALS

When to Visit

There isn't a bad time to visit the Queensland coast. The cooler months, from April to October, are traditionally the busiest season, largely because southern Australians move north to escape their winters. Occasionally, the southeast trade winds build up to 30 knots, making sea conditions choppy to rough inside the reef, but the tour operators know the sheltered spots.

November and December are usually warmer (up to 32°C/90°F) and dry, with excellent boating conditions on calmer seas. The 'wet season', beginning on or around Christmas Day and continuing to the end of March, is the time when waterfalls are at their best and the rainforest really comes alive. You may not want to try some itineraries (certainly not the Cooktown to Cape Tribulation road), but most options are still open.

Visas and Passports

Your passport must be valid for at least the duration of your intended stay. All non-Australian citizens, except New Zealanders travelling on New Zealand passports, need a visa to enter Australia. Visas are available from Australian embassies, high commissions and consulates, and from travel agents and airlines in some countries. Tourist visas are normally valid for 12 months, and cover as many visits as you like for up to three months at a time. Tourist visa holders are not allowed to work throughout the duration of their stay.

Vaccinations

No vaccinations are necessary for entry into Australia unless you have visited an area infected by yellow fever, cholera or typhoid in the previous 14 days.

Customs

Non-dutiable allowances are 250g (8oz) of tobacco goods (approximately a carton of cigarettes) and 1.125 litres (a quart) of beer, wine or spirits, and other dutiable goods to the total value of AU$400, plus personal clothing, footwear and toiletries. Up to AU$200 worth of dutiable goods, not including alcohol or tobacco, are allowed in the baggage of children under 18.

Strict quarantine regulations forbid the importation of foods, plants, animals and their by-products. The quarantine period for cats and dogs (including guide-dogs) is six months, with the owner responsible for all costs. Heavy jail penalties apply to the smuggling of drugs of any kind. Visitors are allowed to carry up to three months' supply of prescribed medications, but for larger supplies you should carry a doctor's certificate.

Weather

The weather is usually mild with little rain from early April to late September. October, November and December grow progressively warmer, sometimes with evening thunderstorms, but even then the maximum daily temperature rarely exceeds 34°C (93°F). Most, but not all, of Cairns' average annual rainfall of 1,990mm (78in) occurs during the 'wet season', which usually runs from about Christmas to the end of March. Tropical cyclones are rare and the region is well prepared for them. Cairns enjoys a daily year-round average of 7.4 hours of sunshine.

Clothing

In this tropical climate, dress is informal, and few restaurants and clubs require a jacket and tie, even at dinner. Lightweight clothing is suitable all year through, but bring something warm for cool winter nights. If susceptible to sunstroke and sunburn, wear a broad-brimmed hat and a shirt with collar and sleeves to protect your neck and arms. Bring swimwear, sunscreen with a high Sun Protection Factor (SPF) and sunglasses for the beach.

Electricity

Electrical power is 240/250v AC, 50Hz universal. Most hotels also have outlets for 110v (shavers only). Australian power outlets are an unusual three-pin configuration, but adaptors are readily available in shops and hotels.

Time Differences

Queensland operates on Australian Eastern Standard Time (Greenwich Mean Time minus 10 hours). Daylight saving is not observed in Queensland (except on Heron Island, where it is used all year), but does apply, from different dates, in the other states across three time zones, giving, at worst, up to six differing times across the country.

practical information

GETTING ACQUAINTED

Geography

The region covered in this book is the coast, hinterland and offshore islands between Cooktown in the north and Hinchinbrook Island in the south, with excursions to the Whitsunday Passage in Central Queensland and Heron Island further south off the Capricorn Coast.

The Great Dividing Range runs close to the eastern coastline, all the way to Cape York, 800km (500 miles) north of Port Douglas. Vast, sparsely populated tracts of tropical rainforest, savannah, semi-arid plains and desert make up the rest of Queensland, which has a total area of about the combined size of France, Germany, Italy and Spain.

Government and Economy

Voting in federal and state elections is compulsory for all Australians aged 18 and above. Unlike most state parliaments, Queensland's does not have an upper and a lower house, which makes for a very straightforward way of doing things. The state's conservative and labour-orientated parties have always tended to be a little more polarised than their counterparts in other states, which brings extra spice, if not spite, to parliamentary debates. Politics becomes even more colourful at local government level, with the countervailing interests of environmentalists and developers often leading the field in a media spectacle.

Queensland's economy is dependent on the agriculture, natural resource and tourism industries. Tourism in Cairns was given a shot in the arm in 1984 when its airport was given international status. The state's affluence is a reflection of unusually high levels of both industrial and residential development.

Religion

Most forms of Christianity, along with the Islamic and Jewish faiths, offer places of worship in the larger centres of population. The best reference for these is under 'churches, mosques and temples' in the yellow pages of the telephone directory. The spirituality of the Aborigines is best explored at Tjapukai Aboriginal Culture Park *(see Itinerary 4, page 33).*

How Not to Offend

Australians are a determinedly independent and non-subservient people. Those who treat them as inferiors are not likely to provoke anger, but they will probably be completely ignored. A friendly, egalitarian and sometimes humorous approach is more likely to establish effective relationships.

Population

Almost two-thirds of Queensland's 3.5 million population live within 100km (60 miles) of Brisbane; the coastal strip north to Port Douglas accounts for the majority of the remainder. North Queensland has a culturally diverse resident population, of which some 7 percent nominate English as their second language.

Italian- and Greek-speaking communities are among the largest European groups, but there are also Croatian, Dutch, German, Polish, Russian, Spanish and Swiss, along with many Asian and various South American language groups. Most speak fluent English, with accents that are not much harder to understand than the broader Australian. There are also growing numbers of South Sea Islanders, including those from Papua New Guinea, the Solomons, Vanuatu, Samoa, Tonga and Fiji as well as New Zealand Maoris.

MONEY MATTERS

Currency

Australia's currency is the dollar (AU$), divided into 100 cents. Notes come in denominations of 5, 10, 20, 50 and 100 dollars, each of which has a distinctly different colour. Coins are in denominations of 5, 10, 20 and 50 cents (silver-coloured), and one and two dollars (bronze-coloured). The one dollar coin is, confusingly, larger than the two. Shopkeepers usually round up change to the nearest five cents.

Credit Cards

Most establishments display a list of the credit cards they will accept, usually including MasterCard, Visa, Amex, Diners and JCB. Within Australia, 24-hour credit card help numbers are as follows:

Left: sunning their buns on Four Mile Beach, Port Douglas

Visa/Mastercard: tel: 1800 450346
Amex: tel: 1300 132639
Diners: tel: 1300 360060
JCB: (Japanese; Mon–Fri 9am–5pm)
tel: 02 9247 6399

Cash Machines

Most banks have cash machines (ATMs).

Tipping

Tipping is not customary even for taxi drivers, restaurant staff and hairdressers, but it's not unusual to reward good service with a gratuity of up to 10 percent of the bill. Hotel staff do not solicit or expect tips, but won't be offended by one.

Taxes

The Australian government collects a 10 percent goods and services tax (GST) on virtually all retail sales. Under a 'tourist refund scheme', the GST on goods valued at over AU$300, bought from the same shop within the previous 30 days and carried as hand luggage, can be recovered at the point of exit – as long as you have retained the tax invoice. Unlike duty-free goods, items purchased under this scheme may be used while you are still in Australia; duty-free purchases are sealed at the shop and must remain so until you depart *(see Shopping, page 78)*.

Money Changers

The banks and major retail outlets will change travellers' cheques, and many hotels will change foreign currency at a slight premium. All international airports, banks and currency exchanges will change most common overseas currencies. If you're changing large amounts, banks usually give the best rates. Travellers' cheques in Australian dollars can be spent like cash in some outlets, but you may need to show your passport.

GETTING AROUND

Taxis

Taxis showing a light can be flagged down from the kerb. Rates per km are around AU$1. A small phone booking fee is charged, and most cabs take credit cards. Taxis normally carry only four passengers, but 'maxicabs', which take up to 10 passengers, are available on request at 1½ times normal rates.

Cairns Black & White Cabs: tel: 131 008
Port Douglas Taxis: tel: 07 4099 5345
Mission Beach Taxi: tel: 07 4068 8155

Buses

For bus transport from Cairns airport to your hotel, see page 89. Cairns' suburban **Sunbus** system (tel: 07 4057 7411; tickets sold on board and at the Lake Street Transit Mall) may be of use if your accommodation is near one of its routes. Sunbus also runs regular services linking Cairns and the northern beaches. **Whitecars Coaches** (tel: 07 4091 1855) link Cairns, Kuranda and the Tablelands with a regular service. **Coral Reef Coaches** (tel: 07 4098 2800) services the hinterland and coastal centres from Cairns, Port Douglas and Cape Tribulation. **Tropic Wings** provides bus tours (tel: 07 4035 3555; www.tropicwings.com.au).

Car Hire

International car-hire companies offer good discounts on pre-booked car hire, with the option to return the vehicle to another major centre at no extra charge – this often makes them more attractive than local operators. The minimum age for hiring a car is 18, but drivers under 25 are levied a surcharge. A national driving licence is acceptable if it is written in English; otherwise you should obtain an international drivers' licence, and if your picture ID is not on the licence, you may be asked to produce your passport.

Insurance on conventional rental cars is invalid on unsealed roads, but most hire companies insure four-wheel-drive vehicles for any road that is shown on a map. Cover for single-vehicle accidents is subject to a high excess payment.

Driving is relatively easy because the main thoroughfares are wide and well-signposted. Note: Australians drive on the left.

Left: fish on wheels

HOURS & HOLIDAYS

Business Hours

Retailers enjoy flexible trading hours, especially in tourist shopping precincts. Outside the core business centres (Mon–Thur 9am–5.30pm, Fri till 9pm in the cities; Sat 9am–1pm), traders tend to follow the demand, and hours vary widely. Banks are open weekdays 9.30am–4pm, except Friday, when they close at 5pm.

Public Holidays

1 Jan – New Year's Day
26 Jan – Australia Day
Mar/Apr – Easter weekend
25 April – Anzac Day
1st Mon in May – Labour Day
2nd Mon in June – Queen's Birthday
25 Dec – Christmas Day
26 Dec – Boxing Day

ACCOMMODATION

There's a huge number and range of accommodations, and you are unlikely to have difficulty finding a place to stay unless there's a major event in progress. Information centres, including the airport accommodation desks, provide free guides. AAA Tourism, the national tourism body of the Australian state motoring organisations, administers a star-rating scheme (one for basic, up to five for luxury) covering all types of accommodation; information is available from any RACQ (Royal Automobile Club of Queensland) office.

When booking, ask for weekend rates and standby rates – it's always worth asking about 'specials'. Specify your needs when booking, and if in doubt, ask to inspect a room before you make your decision.

Resorts are hotel complexes that offer a variety of accommodation and on-site facilities; at the other end of the scale are rough-and-ready backpacker hostels and camping and caravan sites. Also listed are some self-contained apartments.

The following places have been chosen because of their good reputation. The cost for twin sharing, accommodation only, per night, are listed under the following price bands:

$ = *below AU$60*
$$ = *AU$60–120*
$$$ = *AU$120–250*
$$$$ = *above AU$250*

Cairns

Outrigger Cairns Resort
53–57 Esplanade
Tel: 07 4046 4141
www.outrigger.com.au
Penthouses and luxury one- and two-bedroom serviced apartments, close to the central district and attractions. On-site facilities include a pool, fitness room, sauna and whirlpool spa. The prices are per apartment. *$$$$*

Shangri-La Cairns
Pierpoint Road
Tel: 07 4031 1411
www.shangri-la.com
Formerly the Radisson Plaza and fronting Marlin Marina and the inlet, this hotel has great views and a great location. Luxury accommodation with private balconies or patios and a range of leisure facilities, including a large swimming pool in more than an acre of lush tropical gardens. *$$$$*

Oasis Resort Cairns
122 Lake Street
Tel: 07 4080 1888
www.oasis-cairns.com.au
Comfortable 4-star resort-style property with a free-form lagoon pool and landscaped gardens. Has 314 rooms and suites done up in tropical tones. Centrally located, the hotel is only a short walk away from the Esplanade area. *$$$*

Above: Shangri-La Cairns

Acacia Court Hotel
223–227 The Esplanade
Tel: 07 4051 5011
www.bestwestern.com.au/acacia court
Rooms have queen-size beds, en suite bath
or shower rooms, and balconies with ocean
or mountain views. Also cheaper motel-style
rooms. It's just 2km (1¼ miles) from the city
centre and the airport bus calls on request.
The famous Charlie's all-you-can-eat buffet is available every night. *$$–$$$*

Galvins Edge Hill B&B
61 Walsh Street
Tel: 07 4032 1308
www.cairns.aust.com/galvins
Peacefully located genuine old 'Queenslan-
der'. The guest accommodation has two bedrooms, bathroom, lounge and breakfast room
that opens onto the natural rock swimming
pool. Only one family or group is booked
at a time, so you have the whole place to
yourselves. *$$*

Palm Cove

Sebel Reef House & Spa
99 Williams Esplanade
Tel: 07 4055 3633
www.reefhouse.com.au
Much-heralded boutique property just oppo-

site the beach at Palm Cove. Its by-gone era
Queensland architecture is truly charming,
with 69 oversized rooms and suites accented
by wooden shutters, terracotta floors, wicker
furniture and mosquito nets draped over beds.
Lush gardens, a courtyard pool and a deligh-
ful restaurant complete the picture. *$$$$*

Clarion Resort Great Barrier Reef
Corner Veivers Road/Williams Esplanade
Tel: 07 4055 3999
www.barrierreefresort.com.au
Comfortable rooms with balconies; some
with great views, en suite bathrooms, TV,
bar, refrigerator and safe. The huge free form
pool framed by the paperbark trees is a pic-
turesque centrepiece. *$$$*

Outrigger Beach Club & Spa
123 Williams Esplanade
Tel: 07 4059 9200
www.outrigger.com.au
Striking new resort designed along contemporary lines and with delightful tropical
touches. On the top floor are the most expensive suites with their own glass-encased
pools and stunning views of the beach. Large
lagoon-style pool surrounded by landscap-
ing to luxuriate in and a lap pool for work-
ing out. Complimentary Rolls Royce
transfers for extended stays. *$$$$*

Palm Cove Camping Ground
149 Williams Esplanade
Tel: 07 4055 3824
e-mail: hunter_irene@hotmail.com
Ideal spot for campers and campervans, right
across the road from the beach; some pitches
have electrical hook-ups. Bookings are
advisable in winter months. *$*

Port Douglas

Sheraton Mirage Resort
Davidson Street
Tel: 07 4099 5888
www.sheraton.com/mirageportdouglas
A luxury resort on the beach, with over 2ha
(5 acres) of saltwater swimming lagoons as
well as a freshwater pool, and sports facilities that include a world-class golf course,
floodlit tennis courts, gym and health centre.
Accommodation is in rooms, suites or villas with up to four bedrooms. *$$$$*

Left: Sheraton Mirage Resort

Martinique on Macrossan
66 Macrossan Street
Tel: 07 4099 6222
www.martinique.com.au
Only five-minutes' walk from Four Mile Beach, this four-star property has 19 comfortable apartments, each with a fully equipped kitchen. Set in tropical gardens with a saltwater pool. *$$$*

Hibiscus Gardens Resort
22 Owens Street
Tel: 07 4099 5315
www.hibiscusportdouglas.com.au
In exotic gardens with two pools, this hotel has a Balinese theme, with extensive use of natural wood and terracotta tiling. Accommodation spans motel-style to three-bedroom apartments, some with private spas. Less than five-minutes' walk to the beach and shops. *$$–$$$$*

Mossman

Silky Oaks Lodge
Finlayvale Road, Mossman
Tel: 07 4098 1666
www.poresorts.com
Located some 27km (17 miles) from Port Douglas, this rainforest hideaway lies on the edge of Mossman Gorge, which adjoins Daintree National Park. The 45 treehouses and five riverhouses have all the creature comforts you need, plus a spa, restaurant, and rainforest excursions and canoe trips on the Mossman River. *$$$$*

Atherton Tablelands

Mt Quincan Crater Retreat
Peeramon Road, Yungaburra
Tel: 07 4095 2255
www.mtquincan.com.au
Set in an isolated location on the edge of a small crater, these luxury log cabins each have a king-size bed, comfy sofas, woodburning fireplace, TV and sound system, double shower and – the ultimate – a double spa bath with a view! Two nights minimum. *$$$$*

Crater Lakes Rainforest Cottages
Lot 1, Eacham Close, Lake Eacham
Tel: 07 4095 2322
www.craterlakes.com.au
Four individually themed cottages bordering

a national park. Fully equipped, incuding TV and CD player, each has insect screens, hardwood floors, double spa bath, and woodburning stove. A complementary breakfast hamper is included. *$$$*

Pond Cottage B&B
844 Tully Falls Road, Ravenshoe
Tel: 07 4097 7189
www.bnbnq.com.au
Platypus, wallabies and possums are amongst the inhabitants you're likely to encounter at David and Anne's secluded private resort, 10km (6 miles) from Ravenshoe in the heart of the Misty Mountains. Breakfast included in the room rate. *$$*

Cape Tribulation

Cockatoo Hill Retreat
13 Cape Tribulation Road
Tel: 07 4098 9277
www.cockatoohillretreat.com.au
An upmarket B&B with Balinese-style tree lodges overlooking the Daintree rainforest, king-sized beds handcrafted from local timber, and a lovely jungle pool. Indigenous Australian produce featured in the gourmet restaurant. *$$$$*

Coconut Beach Rainforest Lodge
Cape Tribulation Road
Tel: 07 4098 0033
www.coconutbeach.com.au
Set in 100ha (250 acres) of rainforest, its main building beside the white-sand beach, accommodation is in timber villas, with only floor-to-ceiling gauze separating you from the forest. Long list of facilities and attractions including excursions led by trained rainforest guides. Rate includes continental breakfast and introductory orientation walk. *$$$*

Above: cosy ambience at Crater Lakes Rainforest Cottage at Lake Eacham

from Mission Beach. Rooms range from simple Banfield Units to luxury Bayview Suites. Huge choice of activities, including snorkelling trips, horse riding, nature walks, watersports, plus a kid's club for families. Rate includes breakfast and dinner. *$$$$*

Cooktown
Seaview Motel
Webber Esplanade
Tel: 07 4069 5377
e-mail: seaviewm@tpg.com.au
Centrally located motel offers a wide range of accommodation: townhouses, motel rooms, self-contained apartments. *$$–$$$*

Pam's Place
Corner of Charlotte and Boundary streets
Tel: 07 4069 5166
e-mail: info@cooktownhostel.com
A backpackers hostel with double and single rooms as well as shared accommodation. Discount for YHA members. *$*

Airlie Beach
Coral Sea Resort
25 Oceanview Avenue, Airlie Beach
Tel: 07 4946 6458
www.coralsearesort.com
The only absolute waterfront resort in Airlie Beach. Offers a range of apartment-style suites, most with spa baths, just three minutes' walk from the action. *$$$*

Magnums Backpackers
366 Shute Harbour Road, Airlie Beach
Tel: 07 4946 6266
The most central hostel at Airlie has also won awards for being the friendliest. It offers dormitory and twin-share accommodation, and the cheapest beer in town. *$*

Whitsunday Islands
Hamilton Island
Tel: 07 4946 9999
www.hamiltonisland.com.au
There are a range of room types on this self-contained island, all of which are expensive. Choose from the Beach Club, Reef View Hotel, Whitsunday Apartments and the Palm Bungalows and Terrace. Palm Terrace is the cheapest while the exclusive Beach Club is at the other end of the spectrum. *$$$$*

Mission Beach
The Horizon at Mission Beach
Explorer Drive, South Mission Beach
Tel: 07 4068 8154
www.thehorizon.com.au
The views from this resort-style hotel, on the southern headland above Mission Beach, are magnificent. The accommodation is set amidst rainforest that is rich in wildlife, and the resort offers a huge range of facilities and activities. *$$$–$$$$*

Castaways on the Beach Resort
Corner Pacific Parade and Seaview Street
Tel: 07 4068 7444
www.castaways.com.au
Set on a tropical beach, this resort has spacious rooms, one- and two-bedroom units with kitchenettes, and a split-level penthouse – all with wonderful views. There's a pool, boutique, bar and restaurant, and laundry facilities. *$$$*

Scottys Beach House
167 Reid Road
Tel: 07 4068 8676
Popular family-run place opposite the beach, offering budget accommodation in either dormitories or motel-style rooms. *$*

Dunk Island
Dunk Island Resort
Tel: 07 4068 8199
www.poresorts.com
Resort accommodation on a tropical rainforest island. Only a 45-minute trip by ferry

Above: roomy Palm Bungalow, Hamilton Island

HEALTH AND EMERGENCIES

Hygiene and General Health

Public health regulations are comprehensive and properly enforced, so gastric problems from public eateries are rare, and tap water is perfectly safe to drink. Remember that you are in the tropics, and apart from using a high SPF suncreen, drink plenty of water. Be aware of the various dangers that occur in nature and how to deal with them.

Special mention should be made of deadly 'stingers' or box jellyfish which inhabit the coastal waters of North Queensland from October to May. Stinger attacks cause intense pain and often respiratory and cardiac arrests. During the stinger season, safety nets are erected at the main swimming beaches. Swim only within these nets.

If bitten, the sting can only be neutralised by pouring (not rubbing) vinegar on the area. Vinegar is found in boxes along the beaches by the surf life-saving clubs. Get the affected person to lie down to slow circulation, and call the ambulance service at once.

Pharmacies

Pharmacies are multi-functional, usually also stocking camera film, cosmetics and toiletries. They are open various hours, but there's a 24-hour pharmacy in Cairns.

Medical/Dental Services

Standards are high. Australia has a reciprocal agreement with the UK, but travellers from elsewhere will need travel insurance. Without it, a visit to a doctor will cost you at least AU$35 and a stay in hospital will be AU$600 per day (minor treatment for out-patients is free), with ambulances charged by the kilometre. Dentists are expensive.

Crime/Trouble

Take sensible precautions – don't leave valuables unattended or on view in parked cars, and always lock your car. Avoid dark, empty spaces and lonely public toilets at night.

Police

In an emergency, dial 000 for police, fire or ambulance. If you should have a problem, the police are helpful and competent.

Right: rustic Cooktown post office

COMMUNICATIONS AND NEWS

Post

Post offices are open 9am–5pm, Monday to Friday. Offices will hold properly addressed mail for visitors. The main post office in Cairns is at 13 Grafton Street; mail for collection there should be addressed with the person's name, followed by: Poste Restante, Cairns Post Shop, Cairns Qld 4870. There are post offices in all the towns, and stamps are also available from souvenir shops, most hotels and motels, and some newsagents.

Telephone

All six-digit numbers beginning with 13 or 1300 are charged at local-call rate: 25 cents from a private phone, 40 cents from a public payphone. Numbers beginning with 1800 are free calls. Note: six-digit 1800 numbers can only be dialled within Australia.

For eight-figure phone numbers, you need to use the 07 area code only if you're dialling from outside Queensland. If calling from overseas, dial Australia's country code 61 followed by 7 (dropping the 0).

Hotel room telephones are compatible with modems, but you may need an adaptor. There are plenty of public telephones and most take phone cards. All Australian coins can be used in payphones but as they don't give change, it's better to feed in small denominations. Clear instructions are displayed on the phones in English, with some foreign language information for getting assistance. For Directory Assistance, dial 12455.

The GSM 900 mobile phone system network in Australia is compatible with systems everywhere except Japan and the Americas.

If using a US phone card, the access numbers are as follows: AT&T, tel: 1800 881 011; MCI, tel: 1800 551 111; and Sprint, tel: 1800 881 877.

Internet

Internet cafés are plentiful and cheap. They come and go, and trading hours respond to local demand, but there is usually one available when you want it. Some hotels and backpacker hostels also offer Internet access.

Media

There's ample national and world news coverage on hotel and apartment TVs, and the larger newsagents sell overseas newspapers, magazines and periodicals. *The Australian* is the national newspaper, and the major Queensland paper is the Brisbane *Courier Mail*. *The Bulletin* and *Newsweek* are the most popular current affairs magazines.

USEFUL INFORMATION

Travellers with Disabilities

Provision for disabled people, including wheelchair ramps and toilets, is comprehensive at all the major places to stay and visitor attractions. A useful booklet, *Accessible Queensland*, and information on other disability support services, are available from the **Disability Information Awareness Line** (**DIAL**), freecall: 1800 177120. Or visit www.disability.qld.gov.au.

Children

Children are well catered for, particularly in the resort hotels, and the larger hotels may offer babysitting services. Almost all restaurants and hotel dining rooms have high chairs and children's menus. Under 18's are not allowed in pubs and bars. Various sporting clubs, such as sailing and surfing, are happy to involve young visitors; look up the favoured activity in the Yellow Pages.

Language

Australia's language tends towards slightly modified English, which some humorists call 'Strine'. A book, *Let Stalk Strine* (Let's Talk Australian), which tried to codify the local parlance some years ago, focused on the extremes of the Australian drawl and colloquialisms. Variations in accent tend to be along cultural rather than regional lines.

There are a few words and phrases that might be useful during your stay. Everyone understands 'beer', of course, but you will commonly hear it referred to as 'piss' or 'the amber fluid', or be offered a 'tinny' (can), a 'stubby' (small bottle) or a 'coldie'; a carton of 24 is called a 'slab'.

If you are told to bring 'bathers', 'cozzie' or 'togs', you'll need your swimming costume; 'thongs' are flip-flops (cheap rubber backless sandals) and 'strides' or 'daks' are trousers. When it comes to what you eat ('tucker'), a 'cut lunch' or a 'sanger' means a sandwich, a counter lunch is a pub lunch, 'chook' is chicken, 'flake' is shark meat, 'muddy' is mud crab (a delicacy), 'snag' means sausage, an 'icy pole' is an ice lolly and 'lolly' means any kind of sweets. On the road, 'clicks' means kilometre and 'servo' is a petrol station.

Sport

Sport is a major preoccupation of Australians, who engage in it with great vigour, debate and international success. It comes in numerous guises. There are four major football codes: rugby league, rugby union, soccer and Australian-rules football, the latter of which is the most popular. Cricket, baseball, basketball, tennis, athletics and golf all have large followings. There are seven golf courses in Cairns and its environs. (*See also Leisure Activities, page 73*).

Above: so many hats and so little time

practical information

USEFUL ADDRESSES

National Parks Offices

For more information on Queensland's national parks, contact the **Queensland Parks and Wildlife Service** (visitor information centre at 5B Sheridan Street Cairns, open Mon–Fri 8.30am–5pm, tel: 07 4046 6600, www.env.qld.gov.au. Another useful contact is the **Wet Tropics Management Authority** (www.cpa.qld.gov.au).

Tourist Offices

Given Queensland's popularity amongst tourists, it's not surprising that the state is well-served by organisations designed to help visitors. Throughout the region are a number of 'tourist information centres', but some are run by operators with vested interests. The following is a list of the official information centres for the different areas covered in this guide, with websites where available:

Tourism Tropical North Queensland
51 The Esplanade, Cairns 4870
Tel: 07 4051 3588
www.tnq.org.au

Atherton Information Centre
Corner Silo and Main Streets, Atherton 4883
Tel: 07 4091 4222
www.athertonsc.qld.gov.au

Babinda Information Centre
Munro Street, Babinda 4861
Tel: 07 4067 1008
e-mail: babindainfo@just.internet.com.au

Cooktown Visitor Information Centre
P O Box 75, Cooktown 4895
Tel: 07 4069 6004
www.cook.qld.gov.au

Kuranda Visitor Information Centre
P O Box 860, Kuranda 4872
Tel: 07 4093 9311
www.kuranda.org

Mareeba Heritage Museum & Tourist Information Centre
345 Byrnes Street, Mareeba 4880
Tel: 07 4092 5674
www.mareebaheritagecentre.com.au

Mission Beach Tourism Inc
P O Box 266, Mission Beach 4852
Tel: 07 4068 7099
www.missionbeachtourism.com

Port Douglas Tourist Information Centre
23 Macrossan Street, Port Douglas 4871
Tel: 07 4099 5599
www.pddt.com.au

Ravenshoe Koombooloomba Visitor Centre
Moore Street, Ravenshoe 4888
Tel: 07 4097 7700
e-mail: toptown@ledanet.com.au

Tourism Whitsundays
Tel: 07 4945 3711
www.whitsundaytourism.com

FURTHER READING

Insight Guide Australia, edited by Jeffery Pike. Background essays, attractions and practical advice, all supported by colour photographs and maps (APA Publications).
A Shorter History of Australia by Geoffrey Blainey (Random House, Australia).
Contemporary Aboriginal Art by Susan McCulloch (Allen & Unwin).
Wildlife of Tropical North Queensland. A comprehensive book, with good photographs (Queensland Museum and Queensland Govt Environmental Protection Agency).
Daintree, Jewel of Tropical North Queensland by Lloyd Nielsen (L Nielsen).
Guide to Sea Fishes of Australia by Rudie H Kuiter, a comprehensive guide for divers and fishermen (New Holland).
Discover the Great Barrier Reef, one of several books published by The Great Barrier Reef Marine Park Authority.

Right: info centre staff on the move

INSIGHT
Pocket Guides

Insight Pocket Guides pioneered a new
approach to guidebooks, introducing the
concept of the authors as "local hosts" who
would provide readers with personal
recommendations, just as they would give
honest advice to a friend who came to stay.
They also included a full-size pull-out map.
Now, to cope with the needs of the 21st
century, new editions in this growing series
are being given a new look to make them
more practical to use, and restaurant and
hotel listings have been greatly expanded.

INSIGHT GUIDES

*The world's largest collection of
visual travel guides*

*Now in
association
with*

Discovery
CHANNEL

ACKNOWLEDGEMENTS

Cover	**Jeff Hunter/Image Bank/Getty Images**
Backcover	**Kevin Hamdorf/APA**
Photography	**Kevin Hamdorf/APA and**
Pages 75, 84B	**APA**
14	**Courtesy of Cairns Museum**
2/3, 55, 57, 58	**Courtesy of Captain Cook Cruises**
82	**Courtesy of Coral's Restaurant/Sebel Reef House**
7T, 64, 65T/B, 66, 67, 68T/B, 96	**Courtesy of Hamilton Island**
86	**Courtesy of Mareeba District Rodeo Association**
93	**Courtesy of Shangri-La Cairns**
54B, 69, 70	**Courtesy of P&O Australia Resorts**
48T, 73	**Courtesy of Quicksilver Connections**
6C, 7B, 11, 20, 23, 76, 78, 80, 84T	**Paul Phelan**
12	**Tony Stone Worldwide**

Cartography	**Maria Randell**
Cover Design	**Klaus Geisler**
Production	**Caroline Low**

© APA Publications GmbH & Co. Verlag KG Singapore Branch, Singapore

INDEX